P9-DDI-339

HIGHER
THAN THE
TOP

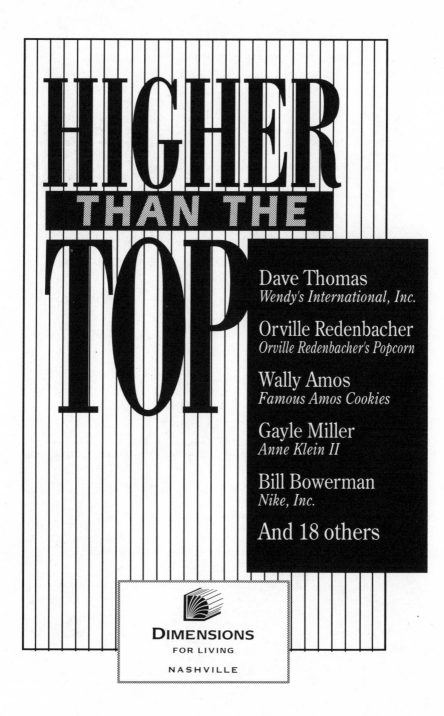

HIGHER THAN THE TOP

Dave Thomas
Wendy's International, Inc.

Orville Redenbacher
Orville Redenbacher's Popcorn

Wally Amos
Famous Amos Cookies

Gayle Miller
Anne Klein II

Bill Bowerman
Nike, Inc.

And 18 others

DIMENSIONS
FOR LIVING

NASHVILLE

Copyright © 1993 by Dimensions for Living. Reprinted from *Guideposts* magazine. Copyright © 1952, 1965, 1975, 1977, 1978, 1980, 1982, 1983, 1984, 1985, 1986, 1988, 1990, 1991, 1992 by Guideposts Associates, Inc. Carmel, NY 10512.

All rights reserved.

No part of this work may be reproduced or transmitted in any form or by any means, electronic or mechanical, including photocopying and record-ing, or by any information storage or retrieval system, except as may be expressly permitted by the 1976 Copyright Act or in writing from Guide-posts Associates, Inc. Requests for permission should be addressed in writ-ing to Rights and Permissions Department, Guideposts Associates, Inc., 757 Third Avenue, New York, NY 10017.

This book is printed on recycled, acid-free paper.

Library of Congress Cataloging-in-Publication Data

Higher than the top : Dave Thomas, Orville Redenbacher, Wally Amos, Gayle Miller, Bill Bowerman, and 19 others.
      p. cm.
      Reprint of works originally published from Guideposts magazine 1952-1992.
      ISBN 0-687-17002-8
      1. Businessmen—Religious life.   2. Inspiration—Religious aspects—Christianity.   3. Success—Religious aspects—Christianity.
BV4596.B8H54   1993
248.8'8—dc20   92-33944
                                                                                        CIP

Scripture quotations marked KJV are from the King James Version of the Bible.

Those marked RSV are from the Revised Standard Version of the Bible, copyright 1946, 1952, 1971 by the Division of Christian Education of the National Council of Churches of Christ in the USA. Used by permission.

Those marked NEB are from *The New English Bible* © The Delegates of the Oxford University Press and The Syndics of the Cambridge University Press 1961, 1970. Reprinted by permission.

Those marked NAB are taken from *The New American Bible* copyright © 1970 by the Confraternity of Christian Doctrine, Washington, D.C. All rights reserved.

Those marked NIV are taken from the *Holy Bible: New International Version.* Copyright © 1973, 1978, 1984 by the International Bible Society. Used by permission of Zondervan Bible Publishers.

93 94 95 96 97 98 99 00 01 02—10 9 8 7 6 5 4 3 2

MANUFACTURED IN THE UNITED STATES OF AMERICA

CONTENTS

A "FAMOUS" CALLING CARD

BY WALLY AMOS

Famous Amos Chocolate Chip Cookies

I'm probably the only businessman in America who uses a cookie as a calling card. When I make business calls, I hand out a sample of my Famous Amos Chocolate Chip Cookies instead of a little piece of cardboard with my name on it.

Fact is, I've been doing this for a long, long time; even back in the days when I was a theatrical booking agent and had no idea that the cookies I stirred up and baked at home were whispering a message to me.

The cookie trail in my life leads back to my Aunt Della's tiny kitchen in New York City. As a boy, I'd perch in front of the oven door like a little hawk, waiting to swoop when her chocolate chip cookies were done. Those cookies did something for me. They were mysteriously delicious, like none I'd ever tasted before. Sometimes Aunt Della would vary the recipe by cutting up apples in the dough to make the cookies softer. But no matter what she did, they always begged to be eaten, and I'd beg for more.

Later, when I joined the Air Force, I was the most popular man overseas when Aunt Della's cookies arrived in their shoe box. But when I arrived home from Korea in 1954, cookies had no place in the life of a man who wanted to become a big-time operator in the theater world.

I worked my way into a job at the William Morris Agency in New York, a theatrical booking company, and I had some early success by helping to bring the singers Simon and Garfunkel into the limelight and booking a little-known teenage trio who called themselves the Supremes. Then I became an independent agent in Los Angeles. The glitter life makes you hustle, and it was fast and tough. I had a lot of disappointments, such as the trumpet player who decided to get a new manager right after I'd landed a string of dates for him.

When things like that got me down, I found myself doing something pretty strange for a man who wanted to be in high gear on the fast track. I'd cheer myself up by making a batch of chocolate-chip cookies. It took me right back to those good feelings in Aunt Della's little kitchen. Following a recipe on the back of the Nestle's Chocolate Morsels package, I'd stir up the dough, drop spoonfuls onto a cookie sheet and slide it into the oven. Then I'd watch the

7

cookies through the glass window in the oven door. And I'd talk to them, "C'mon, little fellers, get nice and fat and brown." Crazy? Maybe. But I didn't care. I was having fun.

Before long, I began varying the recipe, adding pecans, coconut, loading in the chocolate chips. And since I baked more than I could eat, I got to carrying sacks of cookies around with me, handing them out at business appointments. Folks loved them, and sometimes I wondered if they weren't more interested in my "calling cards" than in the personalities I represented.

Though my cookies were a hit, I myself wasn't doing too well. By 1974 my marriage was on the rocks, mostly because I spent so much time away from home hustling business for my clients. And like that trumpet player, some of them let me down. One day I landed a role on one of television's hottest series for $1,500 a week for an actress whose career was in a slump. And how did she take the good news? "That's not enough. I'm a star." Another enter-tainer decided to lease a Mercedes-Benz instead of paying me my management fee. And so it went. It was pretty discouraging.

Finally, in the fall of 1974, I hit a low point. For 13 years I had been trying to make it in the entertainment business, and things weren't working out. My marriage was gone. I was broke. And deep down I knew the fast track was the wrong track for me. Hoping to pull myself together, I rounded up my three sons, Michael, Gregory and Shawn, and we took off in my old 1967 Rambler to visit the Grand Canyon.

On the drive to Arizona, I had no idea that I was heading for a reunion with Someone I had first met as a little boy. As a child in Tallahassee, Florida, I'd always gone to Sunday church and Wednesday night prayer meetings with my Mama Ruby. By the time I was eight years old, I knew all the books of the Bible. But I couldn't seem to *feel* anything the way the older folks did. And as the years passed I left God behind.

So when my boys and I sauntered up to the rim of the Grand Canyon, I was totally unprepared for the special performance that the Lord had planned for us. The setting sun orchestrated a sym-phony of subtle hues on the canyon's walls. Silently the cliffs seemed to move in bands of color, now vermilion, now mauve, now ocher. It took your breath away. It was so splendid, so overwhelm-ing, that I stood there awestruck. All I could think of was God. For the first time in my life I could *feel* Him, His power. His majesty, and those puny feelings of staleness and discouragement seemed to drop away from me. It was as if God had handed me *His* calling card.

After that experience at the Grand Canyon, I returned to Los Angeles refreshed, relaxed, thoughtful. I knew I was ready for something. A new course. Something different. But what? Not many weeks later it happened that an old friend, B. J. Gilmore, was visiting my house one evening. As usual, a bowl of my cookies was set out on the table. She took a cookie, leaned back in her chair and said lightheartedly, "You know, Wally, we should open a store selling your cookies."

Others had made this suggestion before, and I normally tossed it aside as a joke. But this time I found myself staring at B. J., my spine tingling.

"You mean it?" I asked.

"Sure," she said, reaching for another cookie. "And if you're really interested, I have a friend who'll put up the money."

"B. J.," I said, "find your friend with the money."

Right then and there I glommed onto the idea of a cookie shop. The idea was so right it made my heart jump every time I thought about it. And even though things didn't happen overnight, none of the obstacles or gloomy predictions of friends could stop me.

So one morning in February 1975, with all the preparatory work done, I gathered up Mama Ruby (who'd moved to Los Angeles), eight-year-old Shawn and a friend, and we started to clean up an empty store I'd leased on Sunset Boulevard on the famous Strip. We swept and painted and scrubbed, and I put a big sign in the window, "The cookies are coming! The cookies are coming! March 9th." Then I hand-delivered most of the 2,500 invitations to the opening.

In Hollywood, nothing dampens enthusiasm more than a dismal rain. All week before opening day, the rain fell. On March 8, it was still falling. I was counting on a good part of my "open house" taking place in the parking lot, because the shop was so small.

To keep from worrying, I started baking cookies that night. And, sure enough, I began to feel better. I'll never forget opening a 30-pound case of pecans for the first time. I was used to buying them in a 2¾-ounce cellophane bag. Now I sank my hands into a treasure chest of pecans and let them trickle through my fingers like gold nuggets. *Thank You, God, for leading me to work that feels so right.*

After measuring all the ingredients, I heaved them into a big, 60-quart mixing bowl, singing all the time, happy as a lark. *Thank You, God, for helping me get so much fun out of a funny little knack.* Then I began dropping chunks of dough onto a big baker's tray, doing it homestyle with a teaspoon, so the cookies would be just the right bite size. *Thank You, Lord, for showing me that Your biggest gift is the little things I love to do for others.* After I slipped the giant tray holding 10 dozen cookies into the oven, I talked to them while they baked. "Turn out nice and fat and brown, little fellers. Make the people happy." This went on all night, with friends stopping in to encourage me.

At eight in the morning I took off a little time to recuperate. While resting, I listened to the rain beat on the windows, thinking. God gives all of us a special way of getting pleasure, something that connects the brain and the hands and the personality. Could be gardening or tinkering or a touch at the piano. Or needlepoint or high-rising biscuits or planning a party. The important thing is not to pooh-pooh it because it isn't a big deal or impressive in the eyes of the world. You should never miss out on your calling, or the fun of being *you.*

When I went back to the cookie shop, the sky was still a sad-faced gray. But not for long. Pretty soon those cloudy gates opened and the warm sun poured through, giving us a blue-sky summer day in early spring. And the people came, thousands of happy people, jamming the shop and parking lot, eating cookies and swinging in rhythm with the West Indian Steel Drum Band and the Dixieland Jazz Ensemble.

In the heart of the crowd, I ducked in and out, right and left, with my tray of cookies, saying, "Here. These are my calling cards. Have one." *March 1985*

THE KITCHEN-TABLE SHOEMAKER
BY BILL BOWERMAN
Nike

I stepped into our team's dressing room that day in the mid-1950s to find another casualty. One of our best middle-distance runners was slumped on the bench groaning as he massaged his leg. Hearing my steps he looked up through pained eyes. "Shinsplints, Coach."

"Sorry, Kenny," I sympathized, putting a hand on his shoulder, "I know how it feels." I knew too well; I'd suffered that deep throbbing muscle ache in my own running days.

As track coach at the University of Oregon, I had reason to be concerned about foot problems. Not only was I anxious about our athletes' health, but our smaller school also needed every advantage we could get in competing against the Pacific-8's bigger teams such as UCLA.

I also believed I knew what caused most of those foot problems. Shoes.

Poorly designed athletic shoes, I felt caused more shinsplints, foot sores, leg cramps, and aching knees and backs than anything else I knew.

In those days track people didn't have much of a choice in footwear. Outside of the general run of tennis shoes, the only athletic suppliers were two large foreign firms, and their products, in my estimation, didn't solve any problems.

The physiology of the human body had always fascinated me, and before I got into coaching, I'd wanted to become a doctor. In studying the dynamics of running, I could see that a new kind of athletic shoe was needed. It would have to be something with a heel wedge to offer better support, and it should have a lighter sole with more stability and traction.

Evening after evening while my wife, Barbara, washed the supper dishes and our three sons studied their homework, I sat at our kitchen table drawing designs for the shoe I had in mind. When I had the design I believed was right, I sent it off to a leading sporting-goods company explaining why we needed such a shoe. They answered that they were already making a fine product.

I turned to other firms. One felt the new design would be too risky. Another thought it too expensive. And one wrote that since they weren't telling me how to coach, I shouldn't be telling them how to make shoes.

When that last turndown came, I was pretty discouraged. I tried to bury my disappointment in coaching. But a few days later something happened that made me get up and start thinking again. I was giving some new team members a pep talk and quoting, as I often did, the apostle Paul. It's very likely that the well-educated Paul had been a student at the ancient University of Tarsus. To me it's not at all unlikely that he was on the Tarsus track team, for his letters to the Galatians, the Philippians and the Corinthians show that he liked to talk in terms of running: of running the good race, of running not in vain. On this day to my own charges I was quoting Paul's familiar "... they which run in a race run all, but one receiveth the prize" (1 Corinthians 9:24 KJV) and explaining that although winning is important, it is not the only goal.

"If it were, then there will be a lot of disappointed runners," I said. "So I want you to do your very best, not just for the prize, but also for what the *very trying* will do for you. Victory is doing the best you can.

11

"And so even if you lose, you will have learned something," I continued. "Maybe you'll see the need for more physical conditioning, or knowing your competition better, or using different tactics.

"Losing," I emphasized, "can be a real beginning."

As I finished, I realized I was giving myself some good advice. Paul was telling me to keep on running, to persevere. Somehow, in some way, I would get those shoes made.

Later, while driving back to our little mountainside home overlooking the McKenzie River Valley outside of Eugene, the answer became as clear as the green Go traffic light facing me.

I'd make the shoes myself.

I didn't know the first thing about cobbling. But someone said that if you can visualize something, that's half the battle. Well, I could picture what was needed: an all-purpose track shoe usable on grass, mud and macadam, and for cross-country. For, having been a high school track coach, I knew that most schools didn't have the funds to buy a lot of different shoes.

My next step was to visit our local shoe-repair shop.

"Vic, would you teach me how to make shoes?"

He patiently explained about starting with a wooden last, or form, from which to make patterns. "You can make the patterns from old brown-paper grocery bags," he said.

I dipped into Barbara's cache of sacks under the sink, and night after night I sat in my little home shop drawing, redrawing, cutting and shaping patterns until I had what I wanted.

Then, with my cobbler friend advising me, I put together my first pair. I cut out white kid leather for the uppers, reinforced them with nylon, set removable spikes in the soles, and glued everything together with a strong adhesive. The end result looked strange but weighed about half as much as a regular track shoe.

The proof, I knew, would be in the wearing. The next evening when I brought them to the field house, I was a little apprehensive. Otis Davis, one of our outstanding sprinters, was in the dressing room.

"Otis, how about trying these out?"

He looked at them dubiously, laced them on, walked about gingerly, then jogged outside onto the track. It was dark, and as Otis rounded the distant bend, all I could see were those white shoes bobbing up and down.

He returned excited. "They're great, Coach. Most comfortable things I've ever run in."

Then another one of our runners, Philip Knight, a good miller, came into the field house. Hearing Davis's comments, he said, "Hey, Otis, I'd like to try those."

Otis reached down, slipped off one shoe and handed it to Knight, who put it on, pranced around a bit and explained, "That feels good."

For me that clinched it. No so much Philip's approval, but the fact that Otis wasn't about to give up both of the shoes, because he was afraid he wouldn't get them back.

From then on I spent every spare moment coming up with new designs, experimenting with different materials and getting nauseated by the acrid stench of the strong adhesives. And from then on, the University of Oregon track team won races wearing those funny-looking shoes.

In the meantime Philip Knight, who had gone on to earn his master's degree in business administration at Stanford, took it on himself to interest shoe companies in making my designs. He was no more successful than I was, but he persevered too.

While on a postgraduate trip to Japan, he contacted a shoe manufacturer there and sold them on producing my shoes. He raced home and said that if we could each come up with $500, we would have exclusive distribution rights in the United States.

Again our kitchen table got busy. I called in my next-door neighbor, John Jaqua, an attorney, and we formed Blue Ribbon Sports, Inc.

In early 1963 our first shipment arrived in Oregon. Philip Knight, who is a marketing genius, hired college athletes to work part-time selling shoes out of their car trunks to coaches and other runners. These enthusiastic young representatives were able to talk knowingly about the product, and in return they managed to gain valuable feedback on what their customers liked and didn't like, all of which we translated into new designs.

In 1971, with Philip Knight as president, we renamed our company Nike, Inc., after the Greek goddess of victory. One of the office secretaries came up with our emblem, which we call the "Swoosh." All the while, I went on coaching at Eugene and kept working on new shoe designs. Meanwhile, all across America, jogging came into fashion. I applauded this as a wonderful way to keep fit, but I was concerned with the way people wearing tennis shoes and sneakers were ending up with painful foot and leg problems. Now my major goal was to design the right jogging sole, something light with good traction and a clog-resistant pattern. One morning at the breakfast table, when Barbara opened her waffle iron to pour another serving, inspiration struck.

After breakfast, I borrowed the iron, mixed some synthetic rubber, poured it onto the back of the grill and let it cool. It took some grunting and wrenching with a pair of pliers to get the rubber off, but when I did, there was the answer. Today it's called the waffle sole; it's light, has good traction and extrudes mud.

The years have gone by and my coaching days are behind me, but at the age of 76 I still feel the challenge of races to be run. I'm busy with Nike, I am developing a new breed of miniature beef cattle on my farm, and I'm also helping design shoes for handicapped people. It's exciting to think that the right shoes might help the lame walk and maybe, in some cases, even run!

January 1988

ON THE WAY UP
BY LEE BUCK
The New York Life Insurance Company

On an April afternoon some years ago, I was at my desk in the home office of The New York Life Insurance Company when a phone call came from the chairman of the board's secretary.

"Mr. Buck," she said, "he would like to see you, in fifteen minutes."

My hand shook slightly as I set down the receiver. I had been waiting for this call. Now, at last, I was going to be offered the post I'd been striving for: senior vice-president in charge of marketing.

I deserved the promotion. I knew that. For 20 years, ever since I'd joined the company, I'd worked hard. For that matter, I'd always worked hard. My father had died early in the Great Depression, and at the age of 13, I was out in our hometown of Flint, Michigan, making money to help support my mother and my younger brother. I did all kinds of things. In high school I learned to play the saxophone and worked long evenings with local bands. Later I worked my way through college. Not one, I believed, ever got anywhere by just sitting back and taking what life handed him.

By the time I went to work for New York Life as a salesman, I had learned to be aggressive and hard-hitting. And after I married and had a wife and children to support, I was even more eager. From salesman I advanced through many positions, vigorously reaching

14

for the next rung on the ladder, and then the next. On the way up I'd moved my family a number of times, but now I was in New York, zone vice-president in charge of sales in the eastern United States.

In a few minutes, upstairs, the chairman of the board was undoubtedly going to make me senior vice-president over marketing. I would be in charge of all the firm's 10,000 insurance salesmen in the United States. It was the most important phase of our operation. I savored the prospect. Everyone knew I wanted it, and I felt sure that the chairman knew I was the best candidate.

I glanced at my watch; five minutes since the call. I quickly straightened the papers on my desk, rose and told my secretary where I was going.

"Oh?" She raised her eyebrows. She knew that being called to see the chairman meant something very important.

I stepped briskly toward the building stairwell. Usually when people went up to the chairman's office on the next floor they took the elevator. But that was a longer walk down the hall; a waste of time, I always felt.

As I hurried toward the gray-painted steel door under the lighted "Exit" sign, I thought how pleased my wife, Audrey, was going to be. She'd had a rough time because of our many moves, raising four daughters while I spent week after week on the road. I pushed open the door, started to climb the steps . . . and then I stopped.

The thought of Audrey made me think of something else: I had forgotten to pray. Together Audrey and I had learned to take a moment for prayer before making a decision or reaching any turning point in our lives. I was about to shrug off the thought because I didn't want to keep the chairman waiting.

I stood in the stairwell, grasped the steel rail and bowed my head. "Okay, Lord Jesus. I've given my life to You and I don't know what's going to happen during this visit, but all I want is peace. I want Your peace in my life and I want to be in the center of Your will, no matter what happens."

I looked up and drew a deep breath. The sun suddenly seemed brighter, and though that was probably my imagination, the relaxed feeling inside me was for real. My heart seemed to settle and I walked up the stairs and then out into the hall and down to the chairman's office . . .

How long had it been since Audrey had come home from a Bible study and said, "Lee, today I accepted Jesus as my Lord and Savior"?

"That's nice," I'd murmured, buried in my *Wall Street Journal*.

How many years had it been since Audrey had persuaded me to attend a service where a pastor talked about Heavenly miracles? *Miracles, I'd sniffed to myself then. I'm a pretty good businessman, have three degrees and know what it takes to earn a dollar. And here I sit listening to some nut talk about miracles. What has Audrey gotten herself into?* And I'd gotten up and walked out of the session, and waited for Audrey outside.

But later, I'd grudgingly accompanied her to her Bible study, and gradually I'd discovered something different in that room full of people. I didn't quite know how to explain it to myself, but someone who has been dirt poor knows that all the money in the world cannot make him feel secure. Even though I had become successful in business, all my life I had struggled to be accepted. And there in that plain and simple living room I found security; I found that the men and women there loved me just for myself.

Even so I'd gone home confused and a little angry. "Those people talk about God as if they had Him in their hip pockets," I grumbled. But I continued to go back to the meetings, until one night all of my pent-up longing for God broke through and I knelt, lifted my arms and pleaded, "Lord Jesus, I guess I'm not much good. But if You want me, I'm Yours." And that's the way it had been for years . . .

"Go right in, Mr. Buck," said the chairman's secretary. "He's expecting you."

I stepped into the large carpeted room where heavy drapes at the windows muted the sound of traffic on Madison Avenue. The gray-haired man behind the massive mahogany desk leaned across it and shook my hand. He motioned me to a chair. Slowly, he turned a paperweight in his hands, over and over. He stood, walked to a window, then turned to me and said, "Lee, I'm going to ask you a question and I don't want you to jump out of your chair when I ask it."

"I'm not going to jump out of my chair," I said with a smile. "What do you want?"

He sat down at his desk and expelled the words rapidly. "We want you to run the group marketing department. We're going to make George senior vice-president in charge of marketing. And we'll make you senior vice-president over group marketing. Will you do it?"

I stared at him, *Group* department? It was a real comedown. This division, which sold group policies to companies and organizations, did only about a fifth of the business that marketing accounted for and had only one-twentieth the number of personnel.

I felt a surge of disappointment, and anger. But only for a moment. I leaned back in my chair and smiled. "Okay," I said.

He stared at me, astonished. Obviously he had been expecting a different reaction from me. He was well aware of my feisty reputation. "Do . . . do you really mean that?" he asked.

"Isn't that what you want me to do?"

"Yes, it is."

"Well, then," I said, "let's go."

Then and there we started talking about my new duties, and I was alert and excited. Once upon a time I would have been too disappointed to even feign enthusiasm, but now, 20 minutes after my prayer in the stairwell, I was a secure man, ready even for what seemed like bad news.

At that time, the group department was something of a stepchild in the company. In the eyes of my co-workers I had been pushed aside. Some agents came up and offered their condolences. When I said I looked forward to the opportunity they thought I was putting up a front.

In odd ways, I could tell that I had lost prestige in the company. At Christmas time, for instance, when I used to get 3,000 greeting cards, the number now dropped dramatically. All in all, these things taught me something about the meaning of James 4:14, which says that our lives are "a mist that appears for a little time and then vanishes" (RSV). Prestige and stature in the business world—what so many people struggle for—has as much substance as a mist that soon evaporates. I was discovering again that only the love of God and of those who love us in Him is lasting.

Meanwhile, I had a job to do, and soon I truly believed that it was not only an opportunity, but a great opportunity. One major passage in Proverbs helped me in this. "Commit thy works unto the Lord, and thy thoughts shall be established" (16:3 KJV).

I did exactly that at the beginning of each day, placing my plans in God's hands through prayer and then going to bat knowing that He was with me. It worked. In studying our market potential, we found new prospects that had not been contacted before. Our sales force became inspired and everyone really went at it, calling on banks, teachers' associations and business groups that had never been approached. I myself went out and made hundreds of sales calls. By the first year we had sold $75 million in new premiums, about double what the department had done the previous year.

And so we all kept jumping, attending every trade association meeting, getting out there and trying. One of these meetings led us to a prospect. It took many months of discussion in showing him how our policy would help his association, but it paid off. He finally ordered the largest single new premium ever written by our company.

It was fun.

Almost five years went by. Then one afternoon I received a call from the chairman of the board. Once more I felt the butterflies as I left for his office. And once more I stopped on the stair landing for a special conference with the Lord.

Then I walked into the chairman's office. "Lee," he said, "I have some good news for you." He walked over and shook my hand. "We want you to be senior vice-president in charge of marketing."

"That's wonderful," I said calmly.

He looked at me quizzically. I knew he thought I should be more excited. "Isn't that what you always wanted?"

"Isn't that what you want me to do?"

"Of course," he said.

"Well, then," I said, "let's go!"   *May 1983*

STARTING AT THE BOTTOM AGAIN

BY HERMAN CAIN

Godfather's Pizza

One sunny afternoon in 1982 I stood looking out over Minneapolis; the city below seen from my office on the 31st floor of the glittering new Pillsbury headquarters, seemed spread at my feet. In a way it was.

I had good reason to be satisfied. After all, I was the man responsible for the completion of the building. Getting it finished and moving everyone in, in record time, had earned me a vice-presidency and all the perquisites that went with it. After 10 years of hard work and prayer, I had arrived in the corporate world.

Why, then, did I feel so restless? I picked up a folder and leafed through it—a new budget, awaiting my signature. I could see myself signing budgets and shuffling papers for the next 25 years. The prospect was depressing.

I'd never been afraid of hard work. I came from a hardworking family. My dad was a porter and Mom was a domestic. Yet even with both of them working, our family was poor. My brother and

I slept on a fold-up bed in the kitchen of our three-room rented house in Atlanta. But despite our poverty, Dad instilled good values in us. He told us, "Don't get in trouble, don't talk back to your mother, go to church, and study hard and finish school."

Dad was ambitious. He wanted to get us out of poverty, but he knew that on a porter's pay he would never own a house or car. So he took on additional jobs as a janitor and a barber. He once said to me, "Get a good education. I don't want you or your brother to have to kill yourselves to enjoy a decent standard of living."

Many a night, lying with my brother on our little cot in the kitchen, I heard Dad commiserating with people who came to our house because they had lost a job or were about to be thrown out on the street. Ever the believer in hard work and self-motivation, Dad would ask, "What are you doing to help yourself?" But with his soft heart, he'd wind up giving them money too.

When I was in the eighth grade, Dad got a promotion. He was so well-liked and respected as a porter at The Coca-Cola Company, that the president asked him to be his chauffeur and valet. For Dad, it was one of the most desirable jobs at the company. He was able to quit his other jobs. He put a down payment on a house and bought a car. Mom stopped working. My brother and I got our own bedroom. Dad had "arrived."

And once Dad had bootstrapped us up to the middle class, he began putting aside money for our college educations. Thanks to his sacrifices, 20 years later, here I was, a vice-president of a major corporation. To anyone's way of thinking, I too had "arrived."

Or had I?

I had worked hard to get where I was, first at Coca-Cola and then at Pillsbury. Because I had a master's degree in computer science and what they called good "people skills," Pillsbury gave me the ticklish job of merging its giant computer system with that of its newly acquired subsidiary, Green Giant. The challenge was to mesh the two systems smoothly, without destroying the infrastructure of either department—and without getting either staff ticked off.

I did it; got a promotion and earned a reputation as a guy who could straighten out messes. So whenever there were problems to be solved, they called me, the troubleshooter.

Then one day in mid-1979 my boss called me in and gave me another mess to straighten out. He explained that the new corporate headquarters, a building Pillsbury didn't own but in which we were leasing space, was behind schedule and unfinished. And although Pillsbury wasn't in the building yet, the owner was insisting we begin paying rent or he'd sue.

Not only was I to resolve the legal hassle, but I was also to see to it that the building got finished as quickly as possible. I was also to oversee the floor layouts and supervise the relocation of 2,000 Pillsbury employees, scattered around the city in nine separate locations, to the new headquarters. Of course, I was to do everything with a minimum of disruptions to company operations.

In accepting the assignment I was given the title of vice-president of corporate systems and services. The job itself took two and a half years, but we finally did it.

Now here I was, just six months after the big move, feeling bored and restless. Oh, sure, there were new projects in the works, but I wouldn't see the results for at least five years.

As I stood gazing out over the city from my aerie on the 31st floor, I kept thinking about my father. In his day, through hard work, he had gone as far as he could. But now the opportunities for black people were greater. And no matter what anyone else thought, I knew I hadn't yet gone as far as I could. I hadn't yet maximized my potential, as they say. So I knew I could never allow myself to feel self-satisfied.

That afternoon I got an idea. In corporate America there are two categories of executive positions, line operations and staff support. The guys in line operations are the ones who run things, make the decisions. Those in staff support provide advice, information and technical services. I was in staff support. But I wanted to be a decision-maker, not just a guy supporting the decision-makers. So I went in to see my boss.

"Well, Herman," my boss said, "you can probably run any staff function we've got, but you've never worked in any type of line function. You don't have the background to make those kinds of decisions."

"What do I need to do?" I asked.

"You've got to learn all about line operations."

"How do I do that?"

He sat back, made a steeple of his fingers, and said, "Fast-food restaurants are going to continue to grow. As you know, about fifty percent of our portfolio are restaurants. So we need good, sharp management talent on the restaurant side of our business. Maybe you should consider our Burger King division."

"Burger King?"

"Yes. Now, you've got the management skills and people skills to make good business decisions, but you don't know anything about the burger business. So we'd have to put you on the burger operations training track. You'd start at the bottom and learn it from the ground up. Think it over."

Did I dare make this radical move? My boss said my salary would remain at its present level for a while, but I'd lose my title, my new office, my stock options—everything—to start over at Burger King, flipping hamburgers with the broiler crew.

My friends thought I was crazy. "Black men don't just jump from a really good job into something uncertain," they said. "Heck, even most *white* men wouldn't take that chance."

I knew the risks, but I also knew my abilities. Now, as with every major decision in my life, I got down on my knees and prayed about it: "Lord, what do *You* want me to do?" Then I waited for God's answer.

A few days later my wife, Gloria, who had always quietly supported my career decisions, did something unusual for her. Seeing me quiet and thoughtful, she said, "I *know* you can do this." She said it with such enthusiasm that I considered it a sign from God that I was to make this move.

From that point on, I never looked back. It was tough, believe me. I worked harder than ever, and when things got bad I'd pray. Then a voice in my heart would whisper, *It can be done.*

Well, I succeeded. I made it to regional vice-president of Burger King. Then Pillsbury promoted me to president of its Godfather's Pizza subsidiary, and in 1988 a group of us executives offered to buy Godfather's from Pillsbury. Today we own the company.

I often think about my dad. Through hard work and prayer he rose to become valet to the company president. And I've prayed and worked hard too. In many ways I'm just like my dad. Except that I *am* the company president.   *July 1991*

THE BEGINNING OF SOMETHING VERY GOOD
BY THOMAS CARVEL
Carvel Ice Cream

Back in the summer of 1934 I was 28 years old and at a dead end. I was living in New York City then, bouncing from one thing to another. I tried playing drums in a jazz combo, had a crack at semi-pro football, sold radios and appliances. Nothing seemed to work for me.

Eventually I scraped together enough money one summer to build a small house trailer which I hitched to a Model A Ford. I had planned to take the trailer out of the steamy city and sell ice cream, hot dogs and soft drinks.

On a Friday afternoon I set off for Kensico Dam, north of White Plains, New York. There I would try to cool off picnickers and passers-by—at a profit, I hoped.

As I made my way along Central Avenue in Hartsdale, New York, one of the trailer tires blew out. Still miles from my goal, I was out in the middle of nowhere, without a person in sight. I had no tools to fix the tire and no money to have it fixed. On top of all that, the ice cream in my trailers was melting—and it represented my entire savings.

Feeling absolutely at my wit's end, I sat on the Ford's running board and prayed: "Dear Lord, I dream of running my own business someday. But I can't go anywhere with that tire. What am I supposed to do?"

When I finished praying, I felt a little better, but the tire was still flat and I didn't notice anybody suddenly coming to rescue me. I did notice, though, for the first time, a little pottery shop across the road from where my trailer sat. Venturing over, I was greeted by a burly, gray-haired man.

"Trouble?" he said.

"Yes, my trailer broke down." I went into a recital of my woes.

"Look," the man said, "I'll help you bring your trailer over to my yard here and you can hitch it up to my electricity."

Thus began a new turn in my life. Pop Quinlan, that kindly potter, let me hook up his lights to my trailer and I was open for business both day and night. I paid Pop when I could and helped him sell pottery when I couldn't.

Gradually business picked up. I discovered the advantages of selling from a stationary stand. I learned the refrigeration business there, too—and in my spare time I worked in the back of the pottery shop on a mechanical device to dispense ice cream. Eventually I patented the inventions I had worked out.

A few years later I began to market my own ice cream in Carvel stores—and that pottery shop became the chain's pilot plant.

Some may call what happened to me just plain good luck. I see it a bit differently.

I believe that if you work hard enough at something, God will see your struggles. He'll see your tears and your sweat, and He'll care. And if you'll just open yourself up to the possibilities—

which often lie hidden—things *will* change for the better, often beyond your wildest dreams.

Your worst day could be the beginning of something very good. That's the way it was for me.   *February 1975*

ON MY OWN, WITH GOD'S HELP
BY VIOLA CHISHOLM
Designer/Dressmaker

What a predicament—55 and out of a job! For years I'd worked in community agencies, and I loved it, always helping people, some way or other. But now budgets had been cut and I'd been let go. Right away I started making applications everywhere, but the story was always the same: "You're overqualified, Mrs. Chisholm," or, worse, "Your experience is excellent, but even though you have a college background, we can't hire you without a degree.

"I've always managed, somehow," I told myself. Since the breakup of my marriage years before, I had brought up four children alone. God always saw to it that I had a paycheck; I never once doubted it came from Him.

But I'd never been this old before! Or this discouraged. Me, the optimist who cheered others on. It was always my nature to look on the bright side. In my family, people were always saying things to me like, "Sis, what does it take for you to see the rain? A bucket of water poured over your head?" Now my upbeat nature was being sorely tested in a job market that seemed to value youth above all.

Finally I got a job doing alterations at a dry cleaner's. I'd always enjoyed sewing. When I lived in the housing projects I even taught sewing basics such as putting up a hem or sewing on buttons. Working with needle and thread was a talent I'd always had. I called it a gift from God, but I never thought of it as a way of making a living. This job didn't pay much; I was barely getting by.

"You should start your own dressmaking business, Mommy," my daughter Gwenie said. "The way you can sew, it's a waste to be working for someone else."

I smiled. "That's easy for you to say." She was young, making it on her own, as all my kids were by now. And I had to make it too. I sure didn't want them ever having to take care of *me*.

"You can do it, Mommy," Venita said. "You've got to have faith in yourself." She was turning my words back on me, words I'd used to encourage her.

"But," I said, "at my age . . ."

Venita was hearing no buts. "I've heard people brag about the work you do for them. Have you ever had one complaint?"

"No . . ." I did do some sewing for friends, a taking-in here or a letting-out there, even an original design now and then. But lately I'd been too tired, my eyes strained after a long day at the cleaner's, and I'd been turning people down.

"They'd come back," Gwenie said, "and bring others. At least think about it. Okay?"

"I'll do better than that—I'll pray about it." My faith had always been strong. Back in Virginia, growing up in a family of 10, there were plenty of times when things were slow in my father's contracting work and no money came in. But my mother always said, "The Lord will make a way for us," and He always did. I guess it was natural for me to have that same reliance on God through my own years of struggle. But now, a business of my own? I had become accustomed to the security of a regular paycheck. Besides, I didn't have enough money saved to get started.

I talked to my other children. Diane said, "You should definitely do it, Mommy." The youngest, Gwenie, said, "I'll help you, Mommy." Venita suggested, "We can even do pickup-and-delivery service." And my son in Texas, LaRue, whooped long distance, "Go for it, Mom!"

Finally, bravely, I gave notice at the dry cleaner's. "I'm going into business for myself," I said, and even though my voice shook a little, the words sounded great. They wished me well.

Daytimes, caught up in the excitement of making plans, there was no time for doubts. But when night came, my prayers were uncertain. *Lord, what if I don't get enough work?*

We found a discount place to print up fliers, and I designed a professional card: Vi's ALTERATIONS PLUS. COME BY AND SEE VI. CUSTOM CLOTHING, REPAIRS, ALTERATIONS, WITH A LOVING TOUCH. That last phrase was my "plus."

I arranged a workroom upstairs in my house, with a large table for cutting out fabric, my sewing machine by the window, all my brightly colored threads neatly arranged along one wall, and a rack for hanging finished garments. I was ready.

June 4, 1983. Opening day. Our fliers had advertised open house, with a discount for work brought in that day. We were up early; my daughters and their friends blew up balloons and decorated the house inside and out with streamers. It was some festive place! Our minister came to dedicate my new business. We all bowed our heads as he prayed: "Lord, be with Viola in this new venture. Lead, direct and guide her."

The whole street was alive with activity. Venita and her friends played music and put on skits throughout the day. Our signs fluttered a welcome in the summer breeze.

And the people came! Bringing patterns: "Can you do this? I'm so hard to fit." A whole wardrobe to alter: "I've gained a ton, and let's face it, I'm never going to lose it."

By nightfall I had work to last for weeks and weeks; my workroom was piled high with patterns and material. As I fell into bed, exhausted but exhilarated, my prayers were heartfelt thanks.

I worked happily day after day, my own boss. As I finished each garment the money came in—and went out again as I paid bills that had been piling up. But that was all right: income and outgo, that's what business is all about.

Only pretty soon it didn't balance out. After the first rush of work, people still came in steadily for quite a while. Then there was a lull, a long one. Again my prayers became shaky. *God, has everyone forgotten me?*

Well, He didn't give me any magic solutions. In fact, there seemed to be no answer at all. It was as if there were just me, all alone, to figure things out as best I could. My faith strained at the seams.

And the bills kept coming, forming an untidy heap on the dining room table. Right on top was a notice I couldn't ignore: The power company threatened to cut off my gas and electric. I'm sure my children wouldn't have let that happen if I had told them, but I was too proud to ask for their help. My prayers that night were frantic: *God, cold weather's coming and I need electricity to run my sewing machine. I know You don't want me to be in darkness. Help me find a way.*

Daylight came, and I remembered what someone said in an agency where I once worked. "When you have a problem, take it to the highest authority."

So, I went straight to the power company, praying all the way! *Lord, lead me to the right person. Help me find the right words. And bless this person, whoever he might be.*

My insistence on going past the counter people to the supervisor of the credit department surprised me. I was surprised again when this stern-looking man listened patiently as I told him about my struggle to get my own business going.

"Well, that's fine," he said. "But how are you going to pay your bills?"

"God will open doors," I said in a firm voice that hid my fear. Inside I was shaking and wondering, *What am I doing talking like this, here?* But something was pushing me to go on. "When you depend on the One I depend on, you know help will come, somehow."

His eyebrows went up; he just looked at me a moment, and smiled. Then we worked out a plan that allowed me to pay a little at a time until I got caught up, and he wished me luck.

Well, before things *really* got better I had to humble myself to accept help from friends, loans I eventually was able to pay back in full. And I learned that I had to do more than beg God for help. I had to get out and take action. So when I went to meetings I talked to people more, handed out my card. Things like that helped, and for a while business picked up again. Then, another lull.

One day, sitting in my workroom, dejected because it was so *neat*—the racks nearly empty, only a few small jobs waiting on the table—I began to thumb through my collection of patterns. Lovely gowns, prom dresses, casual wear, some of them my original designs. And beautiful lounging pajamas (an old fad I was trying to revive), the greatest thing for comfort at home. Sorting the scraps from all these garments, I fingered each piece of fabric lovingly: blue silk, brilliant red velvet, lovely garden prints. A thought leapt out of the blue: *God doesn't want you to hide your light under a bushel! Show people what you can do!*

"A fashion show!" I said aloud. "That's what I'll do, put on a fashion show!"

I couldn't wait to get on the phone. I called people I'd sewn for, asking them to model the clothes I'd made for them. After a few responses such as "What? *Me*, a model?" most everyone agreed it would be fun.

Then I had consultations with my daughter, made more phone calls to find a place where we could have a luncheon at a reasonable price and added just enough to the admission price to cover expenses. Venita, an expert with make-up, eagerly offered to help. A friend who did professional modeling for a department store said, "I can show these ladies how to look like they've come straight out of *Vogue*. They'll be great, Vi."

Meanwhile I was busy scouting out donations for door prizes; that would be a big attraction. A new batch of fliers went out, tons of them, and more than 100 people came, filling all the tables in the Genesee Inn banquet room.

Behind the curtain some of the models were nervous. "I wouldn't make a fool of myself for anyone but you, Vi." ("You won't, honey, I know!") "What if I trip?" ("You won't. Don't even think about it!") "I sure never thought I'd wear this on stage, in front of all these people. And just look at the size of me!" ("You're beautiful in it. That's the whole idea.")

I wanted to show that anyone could look wonderful with clothes made for *her*, clothes that fit perfectly. Most fashion shows feature fancy, expensive clothes that ordinary people can't afford and really have no use for. I was showing practical things and emphasizing my personal, loving touch. As a highlight, I brought out three models together, showing how the same design could be adapted for a petite, average and large woman. The commentary, shared by my daughters and a good friend, stressed getting the most out of a basic wardrobe by carefully coordinating a few good, well-fitted pieces.

The audience loved it; I could tell by the pleased murmurs. My nephew played piano all through the afternoon and my family sang several numbers—to enthusiastic applause. At the finale, when everyone joined in to sing, "Reach Out and Touch Somebody's Hand," we were all jubilant, especially the now-seasoned models. The bonds of our friendship had been strengthened by our working together, and I was touched—moved to tears—by the way so many had come to my aid, freely giving help.

Many people asked then and there about having work done; others called or dropped by later. Word got around, in wider and wider circles, about my careful work and my "loving touch." Once again my sewing machine hummed happily all day and on into the night.

Not that all my problems were solved; they never are when you're in business on your own. But I figure I have God as my partner, and I have faith that everything will work out for good in the end.

Each time I pick up a piece of clothing I pray, "Lord, help me to finish this work and finish it well." And I ask God to bless the person who entrusted this garment to me. Then I ask Him to take care of me, and He does! I may not have all that I *want*, but He sees that I have everything I *need*.

Did I say I was in business *on my own?* Well, I guess I should correct myself. On my own, *with God's help*. There's a mighty big difference! *September 1988*

WISDOM FROM ABOVE
BY VALERY CRAANE
New York Stockbroker

I just got to my desk when the phone rang. "Mrs. Craane?" an anxious voice demanded. "Did you see what happened to those stocks you sold me last week?"

"Yes, I did, Mr. Lowry," I answered. I was expecting a call from this troublesome account.

"You told me they looked very good," he said accusingly. "Do you know how much money I've lost already?"

"Yes, I do, Mr. Lowry," I answered, trying to keep my voice even. "But we had no way of knowing the company would cancel its merger plans."

"You told me it would be a good speculation!"

"Yes, that's the way it looked at the time. We had no way of knowing. . . ." I had to repeat, my voice getting louder and angrier. Some of these customers were so unsophisticated—did they expect I could guarantee them riches without risk?

"I want to get rid of those stocks!"

"All right!" I said impatiently. "I'll get back to you as soon as I can with a price." Then I hung up the phone.

Then I saw a man from the supply department enter the office with a typewriter.

"Are you Mrs. Craane? This is for you."

"It can't be!" The typewriter was an old, beat-up manual. "I wanted an electric!" Or better yet, some secretarial assistance.

"You're Mrs. Craane, aren't you? Where do you want it?"

"Oh, put it anywhere!" I said.

After the man placed it on the desk and left, I leaned back in my chair and stared at the old typewriter, more insulted than disappointed. It just seemed like one more in a long line of snubs. I knew it would be rough trying to make it as a woman in the predominantly male investment business, but in the three years I'd been in the International Department, I hadn't had one word or gesture of encouragement from any of my supervisors. The present director, Eugene McGrath*, seemed to care even less.

Deliberately I rolled a piece of stationery into the machine—I didn't have time to feel sorry for myself. And yet—if only

*name has been changed

Eugene McGrath felt more kindly toward me, I might have a better chance of succeeding. All the magazine articles I'd read about women in business stressed the importance of a mentor—an influential older man who'd act as counselor and guide on the job. But Eugene McGrath practically never spoke to me! Although his office was only a few yards from mine, if I wanted anything I had to write a memo.

And even then, I had waited weeks for this crummy typewriter. Sometimes my job just seemed like one petty hassle after another.

First, it had taken months for me to get a telephone. Then, over a year for my own quotron, a desk-attached video screen about the size of a portable television that provides up-to-the-minute information about stock prices and market transactions. Nothing is more essential to a stockbroker, yet all the time I had been forced to leave my customers waiting on the phone while I jumped up and ran to look at a neighbor's. It was humiliating!

Worst of all, I seemed to be mysteriously cut out of new business that came in. Each week a particular broker would be chosen to handle all new investors. But when my week came around, the investor was always too big, too important for a beginner like me.

Sometimes I felt pretty sorry for myself. What did Mr. McGrath have against me?

As I began to type I remembered other typewriters—better ones—that I had worked on in secretarial jobs when I had been married. Then I worked only to help my husband and our family as we struggled to establish ourselves in Venezuela, where his job took him. I had never thought of myself as a career woman. Born on the Dutch island of Aruba in the Caribbean, I was brought up in the traditional way, to think of marriage as the only proper career for a woman.

But that was before my husband died at the age of 36, leaving me with two small children to raise. Then everything changed. There were responsibilities that had to be faced, hard decisions that had to be made. Placing all my trust in God, I decided to come to New York, where my mother lived, and rent an apartment adjacent to hers. With her helping out with the children, I worked part-time and went to school part-time, preparing myself for a career in finance. Because if there was anything I needed desperately to know more about, it was money!

Pulling myself back to the present, a large, busy office in a New York City skyscraper, I finally got on with my "prospecting," as it is called: writing letters to potential customers. I was trying to build up my personal clientele, the steady customers that every stockbroker's business depends upon.

I noticed Mr. McGrath coming out of his office. To my surprise, he walked right over to my desk.

"Good morning, Valery," he said. "How about lunch today?"

"Of course," I said, trying to hide my amazement.

"Is one o'clock all right? We can meet at the elevator and just go down to the employee's lunchroom."

"That'll be fine," I answered.

I was puzzled, to say the least. I wasn't in line for a promotion or a raise: I knew that once my clientele was established I would be put on commission. On the other hand, I didn't think my job was in danger. Although no one ever bothered to tell me so, I knew my work was good. Yet it couldn't be just a friendly lunch! We had hardly ever spoken.

As the morning passed I had a hard time keeping my mind on my work. Finally one o'clock came around and Mr. McGrath and I took the elevator down to the employees' lunchroom, making polite small talk about the weather, the market, this and that. The room was already crowded, so we took seats at the counter.

As soon as we had ordered, he said to me, "I'm going to be honest with you, Valery. I had doubts at first about whether you'd make it or not." He paused a moment while I held my breath. "But I have to admit, you're doing very well."

"Thank you," I said. "Thank you very much!"

"You're making great progress," he went on. "In fact, you're one of our most promising new brokers."

I was relieved and flattered, but in the back of my mind I was asking, *Why did he wait so long to tell me this? And why take me out to lunch?* It was nice, but it really didn't seem important enough to take up a busy executive's entire lunch hour.

But by the time we finished our sandwiches and had our coffee, I had forgotten all my questions. I told him all about my children, Janine and Carl, how they were doing in school, my plans for our summer vacation . . . it was as though we were old friends. Was this the same man?

In a few days the strangeness of it wore off and the whole episode passed out of my mind . . .

Until early Monday morning, less than a week later, when a memo was circulated around the office. Just getting to my desk, I saw the stunned looks on the faces of the other brokers. One was shaking his head.

"What is it?" I asked apprehensively, going up to him.

"I don't believe it," he said, handing me the memo. "He never said a word."

"It is with deep sadness," I read, "that we inform his fellow-workers of the death of Mr. Eugene McGrath while undergoing surgery for a tumor of the brain. . . ."

The rest of the words seemed to dance off the page. Then I realized that my hand was shaking. I put down the memo and went to one of the windows. As I stared blankly at the vastness of the Manhattan skyline I felt totally confused and humbled. I had been so wrong!

He must have known for a long time, a calm voice whispered inside my head. He must have known that very day we went to lunch, just how serious his illness was. His kind words had been more precious than I had realized. He had been testing me. Was that lunch his way of settling account, telling me I'd passed?

Standing there, I could feel my grievances and resentments explode and disappear like so many insubstantial balloons, dashed against the sharp edge of this realization: He had never had anything personal against me! Feelings of peace and gratitude opened up inside of me, muted by a compassion for Mr. McGrath that I had not expressed while he was still alive.

I offered a prayer for him—and one of thanks for his encouragement to me.

Dabbing at my eyes, I walked unsteadily back to my desk, passing the broker whose quotron I had used so often. The screen was flickering with the number and letters it had taken me such a struggle to learn to read. The broker nodded sympathetically to me and I tried to smile. He was a friendly and helpful man—if I hadn't had to run back and forth to his desk so often I never would have had the chance to chat with him and learn from him. Perhaps, I thought, I had been wrong about a lot of things.

Recently I came across something in the Bible that helped me understand just how wrong I was: "But if you are harbouring bitter jealousy . . . in your hearts, consider whether your claims are not false, and a defiance of the truth. This is not the wisdom that comes from above. . . . The wisdom from above is . . . pure . . . peace-loving, considerate, and open to reason . . . rich in mercy and in the kindly deeds that are its fruit" (James 3: 14-17 NEB).

For a few days after Mr. McGrath's death I was lost in a fog, my old foundation of resentment demolished by his act of kindness. But I now noticed that most of my male colleagues were helpful and supportive and I remembered that none of my supervisors had ever given me a bad report. Although the problems of breaking into a "man's" field are real enough, I tried to see things as they really were without blowing up my problems all out of proportion or blaming them on other people. It took time, but I came to feel a rewarding sense of security and fulfillment in my work.

One day I received a call from a man with what is known as a "cash flow" problem.

"My income is adequate," he said, "but what with the mortgage, two kids in college and deductions for insurance, I have a problem with cash flow. I wonder if I should sell some of my investments?"

As we spoke I knew that my attitude had truly changed. I no longer thought of my customer as just a portfolio—a collection of investments, good and bad—but as a human being coming to me for a solution. As I listened to him, instead of thinking that he was blaming me for all his problems, I tried to look for creative answers, to empathize.

In the weeks and months to come, my clientele grew rapidly in number, and I was finally put on commission as a full-fledged stockbroker.

Often, when seeming dilemmas come up, I am tempted to blame them on my department director or on the market or on the unfairness of life in general, but soon enough I remember my conversation with Mr. McGrath and the lesson it led me to: "Consider whether your claims are not false . . ." The obstacles don't just vanish, but the cloud of vexation does, and I go on with my business with fresh energy, interest and confidence.   *February 1980*

UP THE CORPORATE LADDER—AND INTO THE LIONS' DEN

BY PRICIE HANNA
Scott Paper Company

I was 32 years old and eight months pregnant with our second child when I became the first woman vice president for Scott Paper Company in Philadelphia. And then, only a month later, I was lying in the maternity ward of suburban Bryn Mawr Hospital. On one side of my bed in his clear plastic baby bin was our day-old son, Colin, Jr. On a tray on the other side loomed a mountain of corporate reports and computer printouts—the "homework" for my new job.

Well, I thought wryly, squirming against the lumpy hospital pillows behind my back, *here I am. A woman of the 1980s. But am I up to the task?*

It wasn't the prospect of combining motherhood with a job that worried me. With the birth of our daughter, Jeannie, six years earlier, I'd discovered that—for me, at least—being a mother and businesswoman were not mutually exclusive callings. And my husband, Colin, agreed wholeheartedly. If anything, he observed, the two seemed to complement each other; the demands of my job made the time I spent with Jeannie extra special, while the responsibilities of motherhood helped me view my office work more objectively.

No, life on the home front was in good shape. Several years earlier I had embraced a strong faith in a loving, personal God that helped me over the rough times in family life. But the life at the office was another matter.

My new job was staff vice president for corporate planning. My responsibility: to analyze financial data and business strategies for each division of Scott Paper and recommend to the executive committee which ones were the most important to support with corporate funds—and which should have budgetary cutbacks. This job put me in the proverbial "hot seat"—in the middle of a politically sensitive and highly sophisticated financial "battleground."

"It's a big job, Pricie—a tough job," the chief financial officer had said with a smile, upon informing me of my promotion. "But based on your performance, we're confident you can handle it."

I was confident, too. Confident, that is, of my basic expertise and decision-making skills. What concerned me—and I didn't know how to say this to my new boss—were the intangible challenges of my new position.

Me, woman of the '80's—I'd be working now exclusively with men at the very top of the corporation. Would they accept me? As an all-male group, they seemed so natural and easygoing. Would they respect me? Probably more than a few of the men would label me "the token woman"—or so I imagined. Of course I was thrilled and proud about my new job—not only for myself but also for all the women in the firm. But tiny darts of concern pricked at my elation. Could I find my way in this masculine world?

To my dismay, in passing months these concerns did not diminish, but intensified. I wanted the men to like me. I tried hard to prove myself. And yet, though I felt my on-the-job performance was good, I was not really comfortable. I was always on guard. At meetings I tended to be defensive and ill-at-ease. No, I was not one of the team, or so it seemed to me.

I'd been in my new job for just over a year when I attended a meeting in the executive conference room one afternoon. Surrounded by male colleagues, I fidgeted nervously and pulled at the cuffs of my blouse. This was an important meeting for me: My recommendations would be used to determine the future of one of our major divisions.

The chief financial officer cleared his throat and looked in my direction.

"Now, Pricie," he said, "taking into consideration this morning's memo, what's your opinion?"

Taking a deep breath, I launched into a forceful presentation of my recommendations. I had barely finished when another vice president, obviously anxious to have his say, presented his strongly opposing view.

As he spoke, I could see the other men nodding their heads in silent approval. In the ensuing debate, my efforts to restate my opinions fell on deaf ears; it seemed to me that the others' minds had been made up ahead of time. A dreadful thought crossed my mind: *It isn't just my ideas the men have rejected—it's me!*

Though I knew I shouldn't take a business defeat personally, I was devastated. Somehow I managed to maintain a cool facade for the remainder of the meeting and returned to my office alone. I stood there, staring out the window. What could I do about these perplexing feelings of alienation? Time and again, I was allowing myself to imagine all kinds of slights and ill will, from snubs to professional jealousy, on the part of my male associates.

That night, unable to sleep, I sat up in bed flipping restlessly through the pages of a company report. Abruptly, I let the report fall to the floor and reached for the Bible on my nightstand. I began turning the pages, looking for words of wisdom, comfort, encouragement—anything that might help me in my dilemma. For some reason my eyes came to rest on the Book of Daniel. Before I knew it, I was totally caught up in the story—and astonished by the parallels that seemed to exist between the two of us.

Here was a young man, member of a long-discriminated-against group (Jews), who somehow managed to serve successfully as a senior executive under three very different CEOs (kings), none of whom shared Daniel's nationality, religion or culture. And here was I, a young woman serving in the traditionally all-male corporate culture. I found Daniel's circumstances easy to relate to. But I also noticed a critical difference between us. Daniel *thrived* in his situation. He was never plagued by attacks of shyness or loneliness or self-doubt. *What was his secret?*

As I read on, it began to dawn on me that Daniel's key source of strength seemed to be his habit—in strict accordance with his Jewish faith—of praying three times a day.

Drifting off to sleep, I mulled over Daniel's close relationship with God. . . . *If praying three times a day had helped him, wouldn't it also help me?*

The next morning I talked with Colin about Daniel. He offered good advice—especially about my concern that I couldn't find time in my busy day to pray.

"Pricie," he said, "prayer is simply talking to God. You can do that anytime. Anywhere. It doesn't matter what you're doing or where you are."

I'd never thought of prayer being so informal. The idea of praying anytime, anywhere—even in the company of business associates—was inspiring. Through prayer God could be with me in a close, intimate way whenever I felt alone or insecure or shy.

"Dear Father," I murmured, as I steered the car out of the driveway and headed for work, "I understand now that what I need during those hard times at the office is You. I put You in charge of my home, but I've been trying to stand alone in my job. Help me today—and every day from now on—to be like Your servant Daniel. Help me to be faithful. Help me to give You all the credit for my skills and abilities at work. And help me to keep You by my side in prayer, not only three times a day, but always."

From the moment I invited God to come to work with me as my Friend and Confidant, I felt better about myself, my job, my colleagues and the challenges I faced. Gradually I began to relax enough to begin enjoying the company of my co-workers again. Now that I wasn't desperate for their acceptance and approval, I was free to see the men as they really were: people with spouses, children, outside interests and concerns very much like my own. As we became acquainted, I was amazed to discover that the men had mistaken my shyness for aloofness, and my eagerness to excel on the job as an attitude of superiority. What a relief it was for all of us finally to understand each other!

Today a large part of the original pressure of my work is gone; I've moved from the "hot seat" of corporate planning to the equally challenging but less politically sensitive position of vice president for Scott's Nonwovens Division. Still, I welcome—and need—God's company as much as ever.

He's by my side at meetings, whispering words of assurance when old feelings of shyness or awkwardness crop up. He's my creative inspiration when I'm faced with an on-the-job problem for which there seems no earthly answer. He's my cup of coffee when I'm dog-tired from working long hours.

Yes, I found the right role model for my career. I'm doing my best to handle my professional life in much the same way as Daniel in Old Testament times.

By trying, above all, to be God's good and faithful servant.

August 1986

MOMENT OF DECISION
BY WILLIAM P. LEAR
Lear Jet

The phone call came while my wife, Moya, our children and I were at dinner. "Bill," one of our company men reported anxiously, "another one has crashed."

It was the second Lear Jet to crash under mysterious circumstances within the month. People had died in each of the crashes. After getting the details, I slumped at the table, staring at my plate and wondering, *Why? Why?*

The planes were as much a part of me as my hands and brain. A new concept in private aircraft, the Lear Jet was an eight-seat 560-mph airplane of revolutionary design that offered the business world fast and economical executive travel.

Priced much lower than similar jets, our high-performance craft had received much favorable world-wide publicity.

Moya and I had put our hearts and souls into getting the first one off the ground. It had rolled off the assembly line in Wichita, Kansas, two years before and now there were 55 Lear Jets in the air, with orders for 15 more on our books. It had been a struggle and we almost didn't make it. Gradually our company had become successful; the future looked bright.

But now those mysterious crashes.

The first had seemed unexplainable. It had happened shortly after the plane had taken off. Ground control watching the plane's blip on radar reported that it suddenly disappeared. There was no word from the pilot, no hint of what had happened. Pilot error seemed to be the only answer, yet something deep within me couldn't accept that.

And now this news of a second crash. I got up from the table, my food uneaten.

"Moya," I said, "there's only one thing to do. Ground every Lear Jet until we can find out what's wrong."

She looked at me with concern. "You mean announce that openly?"

I nodded.

"But are you sure it's a fault in the plane?"

"I don't know, but we have to find out."

"Well," Moya said, "there's going to be an awful lot of fireworks among the company executives."

She was right.

"Bill Lear, you're out of your mind!" went the chorus of my associates. "Do you want to wreck the company? If you tell all the owners to ground their ships, you'll lose everyone's confidence. We're under no obligation to do that; there's absolutely no evidence it's a design or structural fault."

"Of course," they continued, "we can quietly launch a crash program of our own to investigate the situation. But we're under no obligation to make a public announcement. For heaven's sake, think it over!"

I did think it over. I went out into the hangar one night and sat down in the cockpit of my own Lear Jet. As I stared out of the sweptback windshield, I meditated on everything that had led up to the creation of the plane. My mind went back to my boyhood days in Chicago. I thought about the hours I had spent poring over my Tom Swift and Horatio Alger books, learning about boys who invented the impossible and accomplished the unbelievable.

I remembered the countless Sundays I'd spent at the Moody Tabernacle in Chicago where I'd start at church school in the morning and end up in the evening listening to Paul Rader preach in the tabernacle. He had a way of making Biblical characters come alive, just as if I were living in those long-ago days. And stressed all through his talks were the courage and honesty that God expects of us. I never finished high school, but there at that tabernacle I had learned the basics of living.

As I sat in that dark, quiet jet, I faced my decision. From a business standpoint, my associates were right. It certainly wasn't good business to admit publicly that something might be wrong with our plane, especially if we did not have to. We were all convinced that it was the finest aircraft of its kind in the world.

I thought of the years of struggle it took us to achieve this new concept in aircraft. People were forever telling us that our ideas were too advanced, that our dreams couldn't become realities. But when experts argued that a certain thing couldn't be done, I'd laugh and point to the RAF's 500-page treatise on why the jet engine would never replace the propeller.

I remembered the arguments that raged just around the design of our cabin door. We wanted one that would open outward, though everyone knew that in pressurized planes only plug doors, which open inward so that the pressure inside the ship helps seal them in place, would do. However, I'd never been convinced that that was essential. So we went ahead and built a two-piece outward-opening door. Not only did it weigh much less than the usual plug door, but its top furnished a canopy and its bottom a step. Since then it has been copied everywhere.

Yes, developing the Lear Jet had been a struggle all the way. Now, after all the battles were fought, everything could go down the drain, needlessly perhaps, if we went ahead with our announcement.

But then I weighed the alternative. What if another Lear Jet went down? What if more lives were lost? Could I live with myself? Was *anything* worth that?

I stood up and stepped out of the plane. There was only one thing to do.

We contacted every Lear Jet owner and advised them to ground their planes until we could complete our investigation. The press picked up the news, and it caused a stir throughout the business world.

In the meantime I set to work. I lay awake all night trying to figure out what had happened. I had taken my own jet apart inch by inch, studying every piece for a clue. Finally I decided to take Sherlock Holmes's approach. As a youngster I had devoured A. Conan Doyle's books. Perhaps now was the time to employ the great detective's famous principle of unraveling a mystery by looking for common denominators. What common factors were involved in both crashes?

It didn't take long to find that out. Both planes had taken off in a warm rain, had climbed rapidly to 24,000 feet, then leveled off. Suddenly, as their speed increased, they disappeared from the radar screen. It all seemed to have something to do with rain, altitude and speed.

In the meantime, the dire warnings of my business associates began to be proven right. Some of the companies who had ordered Lear Jets canceled their contracts.

But I couldn't worry about that. I was driven by something far deeper.

There was an answer. I had to believe that. As I prayed, I thanked God for that answer whatever it might be. For, as I had learned at the tabernacle, one must believe God *will* answer before anything will happen. So, fired by this expectation, we worked on.

Again and again we went over the similarities—rain, a fast climb (no plane had climbed as fast before), the altitude of 24,000 feet, then the leveling off and acceleration.

Again I went over the plane. For some reason I was drawn to the plane's elevators, the movable part of the tail assembly that makes an airplane climb or dive. I studied them carefully, noting the usual drain holes in them.

Something tugged at me. Could those drain holes have something to do with it? I analyzed them in ratio to speed, aerodynamic pressure, rain, altitude—and suddenly I had an insight.

It was a shocking possibility that by rights should never happen.

I went over my computations again. An ominous pattern was beginning to build before me. Normally the rain water would drain. But at 24,000 feet and at high speed, the trapped water could freeze, the weight of it changing the center of balance of the elevators.

As a result, when the plane leveled off and increased speed, the unbalanced elevators might then flutter, throwing the plane out of control.

All of this could happen only under unusual circumstances, but still. . . .

So far it was only a theory. Now there was only one thing to do—take the Lear Jet up myself, under the same conditions. And, to duplicate the rain aspect, we arranged tubing in front of the elevators to spray them with dyed water.

I went up. When I landed, we checked and sure enough, the interiors of the elevators were stained with dye.

Now to prove the final, and deadly, effect. We fastened two-ounce weights to the back of each elevator, duplicating the effect of the frozen water. Again I took the ship up myself. The jet shot into the blue like a bullet. At 24,000 feet I leveled off and began to accelerate.

The air-speed needle swung over to 450 mph, 500 mph, 550 mph. Suddenly the plane exploded into a vibration that almost sent me sprawling at the controls. It was all I could do to hang on to the wheel. Gauges flew from the instrument panel. If I had not been ready for the effect of the extra weight, the plane would have torn itself from my control.

As it was I immediately cut speed and was just barely able to bring the ship level. Breathing hard, I headed back to the field and landed. As I taxied down the runway, I knew I had the answer to the problem. It involved a simple change on the elevators. A small air foil in front of the drain holes would prevent the situation from ever happening again.

Teams of company men went into action, rushing around the country and making the changes on our planes. Within three days all Lear Jets were flying again.

It took a year before we fully gained back public confidence in Lear Jets. But it did come back, perhaps more than it would have if we had avoided making the announcement. Not only did all the companies that had canceled their orders come back to reorder, but the plane also increased steadily in popularity.

Today over 500 Lear Jets are flying safely all over the world.

The other day I happened to find myself in a commercial airliner. As we lumbered off the runway and lifted into the air, I noticed a small sweptwing white jet with a rakish, high, scorpion tail, climbing past us. It was like watching one of my own children. And, as I watched that Lear Jet disappear into the distance, I smiled and seemed to hear Paul Rader preaching again in the old Moody Tabernacle about the peace and satisfaction the Lord gives through a clear conscience.   *November 1975*

FROM DAYDREAMS TO SUCCESS
BY SAM MEINEKE
Meineke Discount Mufflers

Chock! Chock! Chock!

My hoe glinted in the hot sun as I moved slowly down the long row of cotton, clearing weeds and thinning the growth, leaving just one or two cotton plants every six inches.

We had no help that spring of 1939 on the 100-acre farm Daddy sharecropped in Idabel, Oklahoma, near the Red River. We had to live on one third of whatever we could grow; the landlord got the rest. My brother and two sisters had married and moved away. So Daddy, Mother and I were left to harvest the crop alone. We worked seven days a week.

My bare feet scuffed the black dust as I moved steadily down the row, the fierce sun beating down on my head and thin shoulders. Sweat drenched the shirt that Momma had sewn for me from flour sacking.

I paused and straightened up, relieving the cramped muscles in my lower back. A few rows over, but far ahead of me, Momma was bent over, also chopping, her work-worn features obscured by a sunbonnet. A few rows beyond her, Daddy's back bobbed and moved forward as he chopped the cotton.

A little breeze stirred but quickly died. I thought of the bucket of water I had lugged from the well and set in the shade of a little bush. I'd get a cool drink soon as I finished this row.

I bent to my labors again. *Chock! Chock! Chock!* Chopping cotton could be boring and terrible if you had the wrong attitude. But I usually turned it into a game, or lost myself in daydreams. Today I'd daydream . . .

I see a house . . . just so clear! It's a great big house, all painted white with black shutters. Shade trees and flowers are growing in the front yard and it has a neat little fence all around it. It's my house—my very own—all bought and paid for, free and clear. And no landlord can run me off . . . ever.

We lived in a little bitty house, with no electricity, water or indoor plumbing. We didn't even have an icebox. In winter we'd stuff the chinks in the walls and windows with rags and newspaper to keep the wind and snow out.

Momma referred to us as poor people, but it didn't really hit me until I went to school and saw the other kids taking store-bought white-bread sandwiches and wonderful cookies and cakes out of their lunch bags. All I had was corn bread and a bit of dried meat, wrapped in a piece of cloth or newspaper.

When I was eight or so, a relative left a bike at our place, minus the front wheel. I scouted around until I found a wheel. I greased up a big old bolt for a shaft and got the bike running. That was my first "automotive" experience.

I was in awe of cars. Never having seen under the hood of a car, I didn't know it had a motor, a battery and a transmission. I assumed that cars moved by pedal-power like my old bicycle. In my daydreams I saw myself building a shiny big pedal car of my very own.

My father was a daydreamer too. He would sit and dream about places he had been when he was younger. I was awed hearing Daddy tell how he ran away from home when he was just a few years older than I was and how he had wandered the country, working on the railroad.

We lived miles from town, with only a mule-drawn wagon for transportation, so we seldom got to church. On Sundays, Daddy would read the Bible, and since we had no radio or other entertainment, Daddy and Granddaddy had lively discussions about religion, especially about the end of the world.

In town, we'd heard the street-corner preacher with the white robe waving his Bible and shouting about Judgment Day. So I asked Daddy when that dreadful day was coming. And he said, "Son, no man knoweth the hour. But we're to be ready."

Poor as he was, Daddy never asked the Lord for material things—he believed they were a man's responsibility. But my mother had no qualms about praying for material blessings. Momma fussed a lot; she constantly fretted that we didn't own a stick, and what was to prevent the owner of our little farm from putting us out on the road?

It was Momma's constant talk about being thrown out, with just the clothes on our backs, that gave me a big dose of insecurity— and my desire to own my own house one day.

I'd get that house, because like the successful men I read about in school—Henry Ford and Andrew Carnegie—I'd do something. Exactly what, I wasn't sure.

So I'd daydream, but I'd also think, *If my daydreams are ever going to come true—if anything good is ever going to happen to me— I'm going to have to make it happen.*

Our school bus used to go past a little Baptist church in the hills. I began riding my bicycle up there to Sunday school. When I was 12, I went forward and accepted Jesus as my Savior.

At the start of World War II, we left the Red River bottoms and the cotton fields and moved to Texas, our belongings teeter-tottering atop a rickety old truck, just like the Joads in *The Grapes of Wrath*. Eventually we settled in Pasadena, a suburb of Houston, where Daddy got a job in a shipyard.

Our rented house was like a palace, with electricity, an indoor commode and—wonder of wonders—a refrigerator. Why, you could set a Coke in it and get it out in a while . . . cold!

The first morning, Momma woke me up at 6:30. "A country boy in the city needs a job," she said.

I started out mowing lawns for 50 cents—undercutting my competitors by a quarter. A portion of my earnings went to Momma, a portion was for clothes, and the rest I saved.

After I got to high school, by the age of 16, I was manager of the paint department in a general store. The owner, Mr. McMasters, a small, kindly man, became my mentor, teaching me how to figure percentages and profit margins. I worked hard; hours meant nothing. I was determined to get ahead.

By the time I was 21, I had three jobs and had scraped up $600 to put a down payment on a service station. But for six months I had few customers. I worked from 6:00 A.M. until 9:00 or 10:00 at night, but I knew my daydreams would never come true at that rate.

One day an elderly fellow came in to buy a dollar's worth of gas. Since business was so slow, after I'd wiped his windshield I said, "Sir, if you don't mind hopping out, I'll get the inside too."

"Tell you what, son," he said. "Don't stop with a dollar's worth. Fill 'er up. I've never had this kind of service. And I'll be back to see you!"

I immediately put two and two together and adopted that practice as my formula for success: Treat the customers right and give them extra service. Soon cars were lined up.

A year later I got a partner, Edward Bass. We worked long, hard hours but we didn't mind one bit, because it was *our* business. And we were ambitious. We made investments: a bogus uranium mine (we lost $2,000), a second service station, some watermelon stands, fiberglass boats, an 18-wheeler. None of those made any money. I figured we had to be doing something wrong. But we kept plugging away.

During this time, after letting my spiritual life slide for several years, I decided to get that straightened out. I began going to church again. There I met a pretty girl, and in a couple of years we married and started a family.

And then Edward Bass and I clicked in business with an auto-parts store. It did so well that we opened a second, then a third. Eventually we had 12 stores. For the first time in a long time, things seemed to be going right for me.

To most people, that probably spelled success for someone who grew up on a sharecropper's farm. But for me success really came in 1969, when I finally built a house, complete with white columns, a large den and three bathrooms. Shade trees and flowers grew in the front yard and it had a neat little fence all around it. It was my very own house, all bought and paid for, free and clear. Just like the house I'd daydreamed about when I was a kid chopping cotton. And no landlord could run me off, ever.

I believe in daydreams. Everything we have—art, literature, products of all kinds—began as an idea, a daydream. That's why God gave us imaginations.

But daydreaming isn't enough. It's when you are willing to work hard and set priorities, even allowing yourself to fall on your face (as I did), that you can keep coming back up and trying again. I know.

That's what turned my daydreams into real success.

October 1991

THE COUNSELOR

BY GAYLE MILLER

Anne Klein II

I'm a businesswoman, and I conduct seminars for other businesswomen. So it comes as a surprise to some people that one of the most important furnishings in my office is a picture of Jesus.

The picture came to my husband and me as a gift from a friend some years ago when I was president of Anne Klein II, a manufacturer of designer sportswear.

I unwrapped the package to find a print portraying Jesus sitting next to a businessman at his desk, the two obviously in deep conversation. It was entitled "The Counselor."

"Thank you. It's a lovely thought," I told our friend, and put the picture aside. However, every once in a while I picked it up and glanced at it. The more I looked at it, the more I began to be drawn to it. Eventually I hung it in my office at Anne Klein II on Seventh Avenue in New York's bustling garment district. At first I noticed some of my colleagues looking at it skeptically. It certainly wasn't the kind of picture you'd expect to see in the busy office of a company producing designer clothes.

But soon, I'm sure, it blurred into the background. People in the garment district are more attuned to design sketches and fashion photos on the wall than a religious painting. They move at a fast pace. There are decisions to be made on designs and fabrics, manufacturing problems to iron out, delivery dates to arrange and, at market time, new clothing lines to be presented to retail buyers.

However, in the midst of my hectic pace, from time to time I found myself glancing up at "The Counselor." It became a pleasant respite from the confusion surrounding me.

Then one day that picture took on a new significance. It happened late one hectic afternoon when everything seemed to have gone wrong. I found myself on the phone in a heated argument with a retail buyer. It appeared he wanted to take unfair advantage of us over a merchandise exchange. His voice was strident and my temper rose. As we sparred back and forth, his tone became more demanding and each accusation shot my blood pressure higher.

"Listen—" I found myself beginning to retort with a vengeance. Then I glanced up at "The Counselor." Immediately it seemed as if Christ was reminding me: "Be not hasty in thy spirit to be angry: for anger resteth in the bosom of fools" (Ecclesiastes 7:9 KJV). I caught myself and was silent for a moment.

"Hey, you still there?" snapped the man.

"Yes, I'm here," I said—quietly. "Somehow it seems we've got off the track. We're not understanding each other." I found myself forcing out the next words: "It could be my fault."

Again there was quiet. Then came his response: "Sorry . . . I think I might be the one who flew off the handle. It's been a lousy day here and well . . ."

. We began talking like two reasonable people and ended up with a mutually satisfactory answer to the problem.

Since then, "The Counselor" has time and again been a graphic reminder of Whom I should look to for direction. That picture has reminded me not to react out of my own emotions but to think of what He would say. To me it personifies His message in Psalm 32:8: "I will instruct thee and teach thee in the way which thou shalt go: I will guide thee with mine eye" (KJV).

I have a partnership with Jesus. And that print helps to remind me that He is always there to counsel me when I'm overburdened, to guide and direct my thoughts when I'm confused, to inspire me when I'm burned-out and to comfort me when I'm lonely. So wherever I go, whatever office I'm in, "The Counselor" will always have a place over my desk.   *May 1992*

THERE ARE NO SELF-MADE MEN

BY THOMAS S. MONAGHAN

Domino's Pizza

When I was a boy of nine, growing up at St. Joseph's Orphanage in Jackson, Michigan, back in the early 1940s, there were three things I wanted to be: the shortstop of the Detroit Tigers, a priest and an architect.

Well, I didn't become an architect, and I didn't become a priest, and I didn't make it to the Tigers—though I went one better and bought the team several years ago.

Back in those orphanage days, any part of my triple-threat goal seemed like an impossible dream. Dad had died on Christmas Eve in 1941, and Mom had financial problems and was unable to care for my brother, Jimmy, and me. So we were sent to St. Joseph's, where we were to live for six years. In one of those years I was fortunate enough to find someone who took those wild ambitions of mine seriously: Sister Beranda.

Right from the start I knew Sister Mary Beranda was very special. Lively and kind, her well-scrubbed, pretty face would smile at me from under her white starched wimple. Her clear eyes would ignite as she said, "Okay, Tom. Have faith in God, have faith in yourself— then go out and do it! You can be anything you want to be."

Although I had the strong feeling that she'd support me in reaching for any one of my goals, we both knew which career she was rooting for: Tiger shortstop.

We both loved baseball. She came to every game I played in, and never scolded me when she knew I'd missed a meal to have an extra hour of practice. She thought I had the stuff to make it as a ballplayer, and would tell me so.

Sister Beranda did something else; she started me reading books. In particular, she started me reading every book and article I could find about people like Henry Ford, Stanley Marcus from Dallas, and McDonald's Ray Kroc. They were self-made men, and Sister Beranda wanted to show me that to be a success it didn't matter where you came from or how little you had to start with.

I was a good baseball player, maybe even good enough to make the Tigers. But even a talented ballplayer has to practice. The long hours I had to put in after school just to help pay my way, like picking cherries at an orchard, scotched that dream.

With the idea of architecture in mind, I started college twice, different schools both times, but kept running out of money. Then came a four-year hitch in the Marines.

Back in civilian life again, I went to college a third time—to the University of Michigan—and got a side job at a newsstand. It wasn't long before I was able to borrow the money to buy the stand and to get a number of newsboys working for me. I was feeling very entrepreneurial.

Then one day I got a call from my brother, Jim, who'd become a mailman. He'd bought a pizza parlor called Dominick's in Ypsilanti, Michigan, for $500. He wanted me to come in with him.

"I've got my papers to sell," I objected.

"We'll split the time between us," he countered, adding, "We'll only be open at night. That way neither of us will be overworked. What do you say?"

It didn't quite work out that way. Almost as soon as we started we were working a lot more than seven hours a night. After a few weeks Jim said, "I can't do it, Tom. And I can't leave my job at the Post Office. It's my security."

Carrying the business all alone meant working 100 hours a week. That meant dropping out of college (again!), and that forced me to take a good look at where I was heading. By then I knew I had a talent for business, and if I was ever going to make it in the world, business it was going to have to be. I sold the newsstand and put all my energies into the pizza restaurant.

I made a lot of mistakes at first. First thing I did wrong was to make our small pies too large. Though I was working night and day, I was going broke. So after a few months, I dropped the small pie and immediately went from a $500-a-month loss to a profit. I was learning the pizza business—the hard way.

In the early 1960s the pizza industry in the midwest, which had slumped for several years, was going through a renaissance. I was fortunate being in on this "second wave." Before long I took on a partner and opened a second store in Mt. Pleasant, Michigan.

That Mt. Pleasant store was not a prime location, to say the least. It was at the back end of a greasy spoon. You had to walk down an alley to get to it, and it was so small there was no room for tables and chairs.

Back then, everybody in the pizza business hated deliveries, including me, because they took time away from our sit-down customers. Also, the takeouts invariably complained about having to wait too long and the pies being cold.

But at this new store, with no sit-down facilities, we had no choice: It was deliveries or nothing. So we delivered.

One night, while delivering pizza pies to a dorm at Central Michigan University, I met a very pretty girl named Margie. She started ordering pies a couple of times a week. Finally it sank in that it wasn't just the pizza she liked. We started dating, and eventually married and started a family.

Soon I realized that with no sit-down trade to worry about, we were able to get our pies delivered a little faster than the usual 45 minutes or longer. There was still the problem of keeping the pies hot, however, and stacking the floppy boxes tended to crush them.

Before long we got our delivery time down to 35 minutes. Word got around. Our phone was ringing off the hook; we could hardly keep up with the orders. But I was determined to do even better; my goal was delivery in 30 minutes or less, guaranteed. Our drivers were getting those pies to our customers quickly.

I was still looking for improvements. When a guy came around with a new portable oven, I decided it was perfect for keeping pizzas hot en route. We were one of the first to use it; today it is standard for the industry. Next we introduced a vertical cutter-mixer for our dough. It is also now standard.

We began asking suppliers if they could make a corrugated box to eliminate crushed pies. No one was interested; the old boxes were good enough, they said. Not for me.

Finally I found a company willing to make the new boxes, which we could stack to the roof of our truck. Our volume doubled—then tripled.

In 1965 we opened a third store; in 1967 we added six more. By 1973, after a few ups and downs, we had 60 stores and were planning more.

So pizza was the key to my success. I was a millionaire, a successful, self-made man, not unlike the men in all those books I'd read.

One day the Toastmasters organization called up and asked if I'd give a speech on the person who most influenced my life.

Who was that, I wondered? A name popped into my head: *Sister Mary Berarda*. She was the one who had urged me to believe in myself—to go out and do it. I called the headquarters of her order, the Felician Sisters, and inquired about her. I was told she had died.

I was ashamed of myself, because I'd never gone back to see her. I hadn't meant to be ungrateful, but getting ahead had just crowded things out.

The years went by. We changed our name from Dominick's to Domino's Pizza and had 1,300 stores nationwide. As the icing on the cake, I was given an honorary degree by a college run by the Felician Sisters. At the reception following the ceremony, I expressed my appreciation of Sister Berarda and my sorrow at her death.

"Oh, you're mistaken, Mr. Monaghan," a nun corrected. "Sister Berarda is still alive. She's living in our retirement home."

I could hardly believe my ears. Sister Berarda *alive?* I had been given a second chance!

I hurried to see her. Nearly 40 years had passed and she was old. She had suffered a heart attack, and when I saw her, she was in a wheelchair. Her face was lined, but her eyes still shone with the kindliness I had always known.

She remembered me immediately. "Tom," she said, warmly clasping my hands, "I've been following your career for years in the papers. How good of you to come to see me."

"I did what you said, Sister," I told her. "I followed your advice; I had faith in myself. I'm a self-made man."

"Yes, you're successful," she said proudly, "and I always knew you could do it. But, Tom," she added with a knowing smile, "there really is no such thing as a self-made man." Sister was still my teacher.

Just before I left, she pressed a rosary, her most precious possession, into my hand.

In the days that followed I couldn't get Sister Berarda out of my mind. Somehow, in my quest for success, I had let Sister's first priority—God—take second place behind the faith I placed in myself and my own efforts. So, once again she had hit a home run with me.

I began to pray daily, attend church with my family each Sunday without fail, and even started celebrating the Holy Eucharist twice a week at our Domino's corporate headquarters. And to this day when I'm out jogging in the morning, I'm fingering the beads of the rosary Sister gave me. That rosary has become my most precious possession.

In October 1983 I bought the Detroit Tigers, one of the oldest and soundest franchises in baseball. A week later, I received a letter from Sister Berarda:

"Thomas, I remember the time you preferred to play baseball rather than eat. May God in His merciful goodness continue to bless you and your loving family, and all your endeavors—especially so that the Tigers may be the champions in 1984."

Two months later Sister died—before I could take her to see "our" Tigers play. But I can't believe it was a coincidence that the Detroit Tigers won the 1984 World Series.

How strange. When I finally made it, the most important thing I learned along the way was something I should have learned in the fourth grade when Sister first taught it to me—

the truth of Jesus' words: "Apart from Me you can do nothing" (John 15:5 NAB). I forgot that in my scramble to the top. But thanks to Sister, I finally got it right: There are no self-made men.

Today, what really matters most to me is that I'm a *God-made* man! *June 1986*

A TWENTY-FIVE-CENT INVESTMENT
BY PATRICIA MURPHY
Restaurateur

I can still see the little bouquet of daffodils, just as it sat on a battered table in a rented room on Henry Street in Brooklyn in the autumn of 1929. What a time for a 17-year-old girl to arrive in New York! I'd come from the tiny fishing village in Newfoundland where I'd grown up—with all the romantic ideas that a country girl weaves around the big city—just as the Depression was getting under way. Men were appearing on street corners selling apples. Help-wanted columns were measured in inches instead of pages.

I think I might have panicked in those days if it weren't for the daffodils. My only income came from coloring picture-postcards by hand: it earned me enough to pay my rent, but there wasn't much left over for food. Breakfast many days consisted of a glass of water.

And still, more often than not, my room had a gay bunch of daffodils on the table. I had been raised in a convent where the message preached day and night was: seek *first* the kingdom of God. I think this is what I was trying to do each time I bought flowers. For it involved a real choice: I had to make up my mind which I wanted more, lunch or daffodils, for they cost the same—25 cents—and I could not afford both. Whenever I was feeling especially pinched and closed in by the Depression I discovered I could shake my fears by deliberately "choosing first" and buying daffodils.

By evening, of course, on the days when I chose daffodils, I was ravenous. I would leave the boarding house and walk down Henry Street to a basement restaurant where I knew I could get lots of good food for practically nothing.

But one evening when I walked to Mr. Anthony's restaurant, the lights were out and the door locked. I knocked but no one answered. By now I'd gotten to know the Anthonys personally. I was worried and began to pound on the door until at last it opened and Mr. Anthony's face appeared.

"Oh, it's little Miss Murphy. I'm sorry. There's no supper tonight. We've gone out of business." Perhaps the long, meal-less day showed on my face, because he suddenly held the door wider. "Have a cup of coffee anyway, with some bread and butter."

So we went back to Mr. Anthony's kitchen and sat down under a naked light bulb while he told me the same woeful depression tale I had now heard so often. Nobody had money, he couldn't charge his customers enough to meet his bills, his creditors were after him, he was one step ahead of bankruptcy.

Mr. Anthony kept talking. But I didn't hear him. The thought that was racing through my head drowned out all others. All my school girl years I'd had one ambition: to be hostess in a restaurant.

There was a lull in the good old man's monologue, and I blurted it out: "Do you think there'd be any chance at all of my taking over your business?"

Mr. Anthony stared at me, dumbfounded. "My young colleen," he said, at last, "how much capital do you have?"

"Sixty dollars."

"Why, you'd need almost half that for a single week's rent." He looked at me more closely in the harsh light. "How old are you?"

"Eighteen," I said proudly, very conscious of the birthday just behind me.

"You're an 18-year-old girl from the country, you've got 60 dollars to your name, you're living in the heart of the worst depression this country's ever seen; three times this year experienced businessmen have tried to operate this restaurant and each one has failed. And you still want to try?

"Yes."

Mr. Anthony just shook his head. "Well I hope you've got a secret."

I did have a secret, and when I returned to my room and saw those yellow flowers laughing from the dingy table, I knew that the secret was a good one. If by "choosing first" with my daffodils I had been able to dispel the tight, pinch-penny fears of the Depression, couldn't I do the same through my restaurant?

Mr. Anthony watched skeptically as I prepared for the opening of my restaurant. I made a careful round of all the shops in the neighborhood, checking food prices to see how much it cost a housewife to prepare a meal. I wanted to keep my charges close to her budget. But then I wanted to give her the one thing she probably didn't get at home that year: that "feel of plenty," that taste of God's own abundance which was the answer to the poverty of 1930.

I spent a long time plotting ways to bring about that feel on a tiny budget. Relish trays. I could heap raw cauliflower wedges and celery curls on a tray—the heap was the important thing. Piping hot popovers passed round again and again; flour was cheap and I loved to bake. A coffee cup filled as you sat down and kept full throughout the meal. Really fresh linen. Candles, everywhere there would be candles. And—of course—daffodils, least expensive and loveliest of flowers.

I was counting on those little extras. There were plenty of restaurants that year devoted to feeding men's stomachs. But I knew from my own experience that there was another kind of feeding equally important.

Opening day, I scurried from kitchen to pantry and back again, testing, adding, fretting. My chef was a student from Columbia University; the waitresses and busboys were students too.

As evening approached they circulated the neighborhood with a box of cookies in one hand and a sample menu in the other. It was time for me to dress. I went to my rented room and put on the evening gown I'd brought from Newfoundland, with such different dreams of the city, a long black dress edged with gold lace—a dress for a ball. It was almost time to open the doors.

Mr. Anthony, who had helped set the tables, was folding the last napkin.

On the sidewalk above us we heard footsteps. People were coming! I started up the steps, then, half way, knelt down and asked God's blessing on the restaurant. Then, with a smile that I hoped hid my stagefright, I opened the door.

Thirty-five years have passed since that night, and I have been in the restaurant business all that time. Just the other day I climbed into a plane at an airport near New York City and started flying south. Below I could see one of my restaurants, the Westchester Candlelight, set in a 10-acre park surrounded by gardens and greenhouses. Upwards of 10,000 people, I knew, would eat there on this one day alone. In the city were five other restaurants I had started: I was now on my way to still another one in Florida.

In the plane I stopped to count up the number of meals I have served in those 35 years and the figure came to over 50 million! I thought, as I often do when these figures startle me, that the principle we uncovered in the heart of the depression has proved valid in prosperity, too. "Seek ye first the kingdom of God" (Matthew 6:33 KJV), Christ said. Afterwards, He promised, a real abundance would follow.   *May 1965*

HOW TO PUT WAITING TO WORK FOR YOU
THOMAS A. MURPHY
General Motors

Three times in my life I've found myself detoured by circumstances beyond my control. Each experience was a trial. I felt frustrated and helpless. It was only later that I realized that I had learned something each time—something that helped me in later life.

I was 16 when I graduated from high school in 1932. With the Depression at its height, college seemed out of the question. The only job I could land was one my father got me in a Chicago icehouse. I became a "vault man," the guy who stacks 400-pound cakes of ice on end. It was exhausting work, the kind of labor that made my bones cry out at the end of the day, and not only that, the work was only available during the summer.

For three summers I scratched away trying to save money. The winters were long and frustrating—no work, no prospects. One winter I took courses in typing and bookkeeping. It passed the time, but it didn't get me a job. At home, I spent most of my time complaining.

My mother, a staunch Catholic whose spiritual influence I can still feel, would look at me and say, "The Lord is making you wait for a reason. One day you'll see."

During my third summer at the icehouse, a fellow worker said to me, "You know, you are going to be breaking your back for the rest of your life on this job unless you do something about it."

"I've tried to get another job," I said, "but I can't find one."

"You need more education," he said.

I shrugged. "Well, I can't afford that."

"That's bunk," he said. "I earn enough here in the summertime to put myself through the University of Illinois."

I looked into it and found that with my savings and my earnings that summer, I had enough money to at least get started, and I signed up for a business course.

53

That fall I saw the value of my mother's words. Two years before, I wasn't mature enough for college and didn't have the required incentive. Now, with some hard work behind me, I found I had the desire to tackle studying, something I didn't have when I finished high school. Also, the typing and bookkeeping proved invaluable to me. I was able to earn extra money typing friends' term papers and the bookkeeping gave me a foundation in accounting, my major. And the delay had given me the opportunity to set my goals and see how much I wanted to go to college.

World War II presented me with another test of time. My wife, Sis, and I were parents of a little girl. I was working for General Motors, a company I joined right after graduating from Illinois in 1938. Then suddenly I was drafted into service. Like many young men I was stripped of my wife, my child and my job all at once. The thought of facing such a long time away from everything filled me with anxiety. I remember telling a supply-school instructor how I felt.

"Relax, Murph," he said. "Take each day at a time."

I found, when I did, that time went faster. What's more, I actually found the time beneficial. Working for GM before the war, I had wondered if it was really the place for me. Did I want something else? Another type of job, another company? Three years away from GM let me ponder my future thoroughly. Once again, I was given time to pause and reflect. When I returned home in 1946, I was ready to make a decision—I wanted to return to GM.

Almost ten years later, in 1953, I faced the third test. We now had three children, and we were living in New York City, where I was still working for GM. My job was demanding, but I loved it. Then, in October, it was discovered that I had a rare virus in my intestinal tract.

"You'll have to be in the hospital for three months and then three months at home after that," the doctor said.

His words rocked me. Lying in bed in Roosevelt Hospital, I not only felt bored, but also felt sorry for myself. Why did I have to miss out on everything? As Christmas approached, I was still in the hospital and still feeling depressed. Suddenly the door to my room swung open and in came Sis and our three kids. They jumped up on my bed, hugged me and started handing me gifts. Suddenly I realized with a tremendous surge of gratitude how much closer we had become as a family since my illness.

When Sis and the children finally left, my eyes were full of tears, but I was no longer resenting the illness and the period of recuperation that lay ahead. I saw an opportunity for all of us to rediscover what we really meant to one another as individuals and as a family.

And that's the way it worked out. Before that, because of my long hours at work and frequent business trips, our times together had been far too short. Now I was seeing them every day, asking the children questions I'd not had time to ask before, getting to know them as individuals.

Surely everyone has been burdened by an unwelcome span of time that seems too long to get through. But I think now that the Lord gives us these waiting periods for a reason—so that we may use them as rest stops to learn more about ourselves. When we accept these delays and detours as signals of God's plans for us, He will show us eventually how to use them.

My mother was right when she said, "One day you'll see."

February 1977

A NEW MEASURE FOR SUCCESS

BY ANN PERSON

Stretch and Sew

Are you a person—middle-aged, perhaps—who sometimes wonders if life may be passing you by? Who occasionally feels that you haven't made the most of your talents and abilities? Who views your past as insignificant, and the future as, well, rather uncertain?

If you are, I understand how you feel—because once I was just such a person.

In October 1965, I lay flat on my back in the tuberculosis ward of Oregon's state hospital. Ominous black shadows on an X-ray of my lungs had put me there.

I was feeling sorry for myself—and with good reason. Just five years ago my husband, Herb, had suffered a severe back injury that forced him to give up a successful logging career for something less strenuous. With three teen-age daughters to raise, we were practically destitute following a succession of failed business ventures. And now, these grim X-rays.

Bleakly, I stared up at the ceiling. My roommate, a middle-aged housewife like myself, was terribly ill. The tiny room was filled with the sound of her shallow breathing.

I closed my eyes to shut out the dismal scene, but the world inside me was even worse. With my illness had come depression.

I realized that now, with my life in peril, I didn't have much to show for the past 40 years. I had frittered my adulthood away; dabbling in everything, but committing myself to nothing.

As a child—ever since the day my mother took me aside, fitted me with my own porcelain thimble, and guided my hands as I stitched my first doll's dress—I was sure I would grow up to be a world-famous fashion designer. And for many years, with a youngster's unflagging enthusiasm, I pursued my goal. I went to college at the University of Oregon, excelled in art, and later taught small classes in painting, crafts and sewing.

But somewhere along the way—perhaps with the added responsibilities and altered priorities that come with marriage and motherhood—my enthusiasm waned and my dream of a glamorous career faded. My life, once full of vitality and purpose, became lackluster and drab. Even my health began to decline.

And here I was.

Never had I felt so alone and empty—and scared. I'd never considered myself a very religious person; but then, I'd never really needed God. Now, I did. And the time had come to let Him know.

At first I didn't know what to say or how to say it; I couldn't remember when I'd last tried to pray. But soon the words, like tears, came spilling out from my heart.

"Lord," I whispered, "I'm scared. If You'll just get me out of this, I promise I'll do something worthwhile with my life. I know I can't do it without Your help. You've got to show me the way. But give me a chance, Lord, and I'll be willing."

There was, in the silence that followed, an indescribable feeling of comfort. I slept peacefully that afternoon, secure in knowing that by turning the situation over to God, I had done everything I could.

When I awoke, I was startled to see eight doctors circled around my bed, speaking to one another in hushed voices. Noticing that I was awake, they fell silent. Finally one of them cleared his throat and shifted his weight uneasily.

"Mrs. Person," he began with some hesitation, "there seems to be a problem with your X-rays."

My mind reeled with confusion and fright.

"It seems," the doctor continued, "that your X-rays have been misread. The dark areas we originally diagnosed as tuberculosis are actually patches of scar tissue from asthma you had as a child. There's nothing to worry about, Mrs. Person. In fact, you can go home."

Home! I couldn't believe it.

Back home with Herb and the girls, I felt rejuvenated—excited, somehow, about what the future held in store. Remembering my prayer, I felt confident that I would find my niche soon. So, the next year found me teaching everything from oil painting and picture framing to resin casting and furniture antiquing.

More than anything, though, I enjoyed teaching sewing. It was in my sewing classes that I felt most strongly my old enthusiasm bubbling up inside me. Students would often come up after class and tell me they'd never felt so motivated.

One day, an appreciative student sent me a huge carton of knit fabric remnants from one of the many mill-end factory outlets in the area. I must admit I received the gift with mixed feelings. Knits, at that time, were new on the market and virtually unknown to most home seamstresses. Those who were familiar with the fabric considered it difficult, if not impossible, to work with. Countless times, I'd heard friends complain how knits bagged, sagged and raveled hopelessly.

Still, the riot of colors and textures peeking out from that box were irresistible. "Try me," they seemed to say, like a basket of fresh-cut flowers just waiting to be selected, snipped and artfully fashioned in a beautiful bouquet. I pulled out a large kelly green remnant, sat down at my machine and began experimenting. Once I started, it became difficult to stop. I felt a tingle of excitement as one discovery followed another.

The best results, I learned, came from using big stitches, stretching the fabric as I sewed. Since there were no commercial patterns for knits available, we searched our closets for old knit clothing to take apart and study. Then, using rolls of butcher paper, I began designing originals. The results were amazing: tops that could be whipped up in 15 minutes, slacks guaranteed a perfect fit.

Word spread, and before I knew it, my classes were devoted entirely to my new "stretch and sew" method with knits. Just when I was sure I must have taught every interested person in Eugene, I received a phone call from a woman in Roseburg, a small town 70 miles to the south. Would I be willing, she wondered, to drive down and demonstrate my techniques to a few of her friends? Do it, a small voice urged, and I accepted. When I arrived there, 70 ladies were waiting. And that one session initiated a chain of classes that kept me on a 500-mile, statewide weekly circuit for the remainder of the year.

Traveling over Oregon's back roads in my little Nash Rambler, there was plenty of time for quiet thought. It was becoming apparent that students in my classes were learning much more than how to sew with knits. Through accomplishments as simple as making and wearing their own skirts, or surprising their husbands with a pair of perfect-fitting pants at half the cost of ready-made brands, many women were gaining a sense of self-worth and personal achievement they had never experienced before. We often used class time to discuss the importance of making the most of your talents and abilities; of living up to your potential through setting specific goals, making a plan, and following through. As a result of this sharing, many close friendships developed and classes often became like small families. To bring both the joy of self-expression plus financial savings to hundreds of women—and to love every minute of it—was tremendously exciting.

Indeed, I was on fire with an enthusiasm for my work and life that I hadn't known since childhood, and I knew without a doubt that the source of this vitality was God. For the first time in my life, I was finally doing what I should be doing. I had found my niche. I often prayed as I drove, thanking the Lord for showing me His will, and asking Him for continued strength and guidance.

He never let me down.

In February 1967, Herb and I copyrighted the name "Stretch and Sew," and I began training and licensing others to conduct the "Basic Eight" series of lessons. Six months later, in downtown Eugene, we opened the first Stretch and Sew Center, where classes took place and exclusive Stretch and Sew knit fabrics, notions and patterns were sold. With the help of my family, I put together one of the first books ever published about sewing with knits featuring easy-to-understand language and snapshots of Herb and the girls modeling finished garments. Incredibly, the book, *Stretch & Sew,* sold more than a million copies, and its success led to a five-year national television series called *Sewing with Ann Person.*

It was Herb, with his strong marketing and management sense, who came up with the idea of the franchised Stretch and Sew Sewing Center system, and in 1969 we sold our first franchise. Today there are centers throughout the U.S. and Canada, where millions of women are learning to sew—and more—the Stretch and Sew way.

It's an exciting and glamorous life, to be sure. But the most rewarding aspect of my career remains the people who are helped. Once, at the close of a workshop in a Midwestern city, a small woman came up to me.

"Ann," she said quietly, "I'm a widow. For years after my husband died, I was alone and desperate. I didn't know who I was; I didn't want to live. I signed up for your classes just to pass the time—but through them I gained a sense of self-worth I never had. I learned how to set goals and make decisions. I made friends. It was just the boost I needed, and I just want to thank you . . . and thank God."

She drew me close and gave me a hug.

"Yes," I said as I hugged her back, "let's thank God. Because without Him, none of it would ever have happened!"

October 1978

THE FUNNY-LOOKING FARMER WITH THE FUNNY-SOUNDING NAME

BY ORVILLE REDENBACHER

Orville Redenbacher's Gourmet Popping Corn

The man behind the desk listened to my sales pitch with that look people get when they think you're trying to sell them stock in a phony gold mine.

Pushing my sample jar of Red Bow popcorn back at me, he smiled politely. "I don't care how good you say this is, Orville. Popcorn is popcorn. Folks aren't going to pay more for yours."

"But . . ." I started to explain, then ruefully shook my head, picked up my sample and trudged out of the regional food processor's office. I knew it was useless to talk any further. He was the umpteenth prospect to turn down the new, improved popcorn that had taken me years to develop. No one seemed to want it.

I got into my car and gloomily drove through the Indiana countryside toward my office in Valparaiso. Was I, at the age of 63, pursuing a foolish dream?

My eye caught a roadside stand, bringing memories of the time I sold fresh produce door-to-door as a farm boy in Indiana. Back then, to help make ends meet, I would traipse 15 miles from our farm near the town of Brazil to Terre Haute twice a week to sell our fruit, vegetables, eggs and dressed chickens. But even then, peddling popping corn was my main interest. I grew an acre of it as a 4-H project in which I tried year after year to come up with a better variety.

Maybe I liked popcorn so much because every night Dad would pop a batch in a long-handled wire popper in the fireplace or on the potbellied stove; I loved its warm homey aroma. In those days, especially during World War I, when schoolmates made fun of my German-sounding last name, I found solace in my family, who gathered together in front of the fire each evening.

I smiled to myself. As a kid I wasn't a bad salesman, selling my popping corn in Brazil and Terre Haute, where grocery stores would display it in bushel baskets on their wooden floors. But why couldn't I sell it now, in 1970, after all these years of perfecting it?

I turned into the driveway of Chester Hybrids, the firm I owned with Charlie Bowman. Both of us had gone to Purdue University (where I majored in agronomy, played the sousaphone in the marching band and won a letter in track). I had teamed up with Charlie in 1952. Before that, I had been a county agricultural agent, then manager of the 12,000-acre Princeton Farms, where I worked with liquid nitrogen and started breeding hybrid popcorn seed.

Charlie concentrated on the engineering end of our business, such as grain storage and drying, and irrigation systems. I spent most of my time on fertilizers and continuing the hybridizing of a better popping corn. This was a new concept, for popping corn hadn't really changed much in 5,000 years. Even the popcorn the Iroquois Indians introduced to the colonists wasn't much different from what was on grocery store shelves. Finally, with the help of breeding expert Carl Hartman, plus 40 generations of crossbred popcorn, we came up with a superior Snowflake variety that, when popped, was lighter and fluffier.

The Indians thought popcorn popped because a demon lived inside the kernel; when heated, the demon became irate and exploded in anger. Actually, moisture inside turns to steam and literally blasts the kernel apart. Our secret was to dry the corn carefully and slowly to maintain an exact moisture level—13.25 percent—in each kernel, making for nearly 100 percent popability. This helped eliminate the tooth-crunching unpopped grains I call shy ones.

Selling Red Bow popcorn, however, was another story. For four years I wore out car tires and shoe leather going from farmer to processor to retailer. Farmers didn't want it as seed corn because it yielded less per acre. Every processor had the same negative reaction as the one I had just visited. And the retailers? "There are over eighty different brands of popcorn on the market," snorted one chain-store buyer. "We don't have room for another, especially when it costs two and a half times as much."

That night in 1970 I didn't even feel like popping my usual treat. Ten years down the drain. Maybe I had better stick to seed and fertilizer, I thought. Although I'd been successful in developing my new popping corn, now I evidently had no talent for selling it.

Talent. I thought about that for a long time—and what I had done with my abilities since I was young. Mom had talked about talents. When I'd practice my cornet at home as a youngster, she would wince at my bleating. "God gave you your share of talents, Son, but playing the cornet is not one of them."

Yes, God *had* given me talents. I believed they were from Him. I'd even taught about talents as a Sunday-school teacher. Something from Sunday-school teaching tickled my memory, something about seeking advisers. I picked up our Bible and riffled through its pages. Yes, there it was, Proverbs 24:6: "For by wise guidance you can wage your war, and in abundance of counselors there is victory" (*RSV*).

Of course. Charlie and I were farmers. We ran a good local business. But what did we know about the ins and outs of big-time marketing? I decided it was time to get my ego out of the way and admit someone else might be of help.

I began to ask around for the name of a good marketing company. A few days later I traveled to Chicago to seek guidance from my chosen counselors, the advertising and marketing firm of Gerson, Howe and Johnson, then in the Wrigley Building. I found myself at a table with two young copywriters, a retailing expert and Mr. Gerson, the president.

"Talk to us about popcorn," he said.

I talked on for about three hours, feeling foolish while they just listened.

"Come back next week," they said, "and we'll have something for you."

The following week I returned wondering what great marketing scheme they had come up with.

"We think you should call it Orville Redenbacher's Gourmet Popping Corn."

I stared at them, dumbfounded.

"Golly, no," I gasped, "Redenbacher is such a . . . funny name." I remembered those kids giggling back in Indiana.

"That's the point. People will love it."

I drove back to Valparaiso wryly thinking we had paid $13,000 for someone to come up with the same name my mother had come up with when I was born.

Our marketing counselors also recommended we put my picture on the label, which I thought was another mistake. That proverb had better be right, I thought, beginning to question the wisdom of counselors. If people had balked at the price before, what would they say about a funny name and funny face?

There was one way to find out. I would package some as the counselors had recommended and then test-market it.

On my own, I decided to approach the biggest retailer in the area, Marshall Field's in Chicago. I found out the name of the manager of their seventh-floor gourmet food department and sent a case of our newly labeled product to his home, but I did not enclose a note or return address. A month later I phoned. "Did you like it?" I asked.

"Like it?" he answered. "We want to stock it!"

It was a sizable order. I loaded it into our pickup truck and drove it in to Chicago as the sun was coming up over Lake Michigan. There I delivered it to Marshall Field's big State and Randolph Street store's loading dock. As an extra gimmick, I offered to autograph jars.

Marshall Field's took the idea and ran with it. They published newspaper ads, and I was there three days getting writer's cramp. Eyewitness News came over and ran coverage on their evening programs. That started the ball rolling with more news elsewhere.

In track I was told, "When you're out in front, you'd better keep running." So I ran the wheels off that pickup driving up to Byerly's around Minneapolis, one of these super groceries with carpets all over, and then out to Churchill's in Toledo. In a way I felt like I was peddling my popcorn back in Terre Haute, only this time I was filling warehouse shelves, not bushel baskets.

When folks discovered it truly was an improved popping corn, we could hardly keep up with orders. Today Orville Redenbacher's Gourmet Popping Corn is a product of Hunt-Wesson Foods. Part of the deal was that I would still help them sell it by appearing on TV commercials.

Well, I'm grateful for the "wise guidance" of an "abundance of counselors" as the Bible puts it, though I'm still befuddled. What do I, at age 82, know about selling popcorn on television? I'm just a funny-looking farmer with a funny-sounding name. But I still think my popping corn is the best.   *January 1990*

NOT BY BREAD ALONE
BY MARGARET RUDKIN
Pepperidge Farm

There's an old Irish saying: "God broadens the back to bear the burden." Grandmother used to quote this proverb each time we launched some new project. "You children have talent," she would say. "Don't be afraid to step out. You won't be alone."

I never had to learn exactly what Grandmother meant until the day my husband, Henry, and I first heard low, gurgling sounds come from our son's chest. The child had asthma: We were on the threshold of needing broader backs than we had ever imagined necessary.

For seven years Henry and I went through torture, listening to this little boy struggle for breath during the attacks. We spent half our time following doctors' instructions, but there seemed to be nothing we could do except pray.

Finally, we made rules for ourselves: no more doctors, no more "cures." But, of course, that didn't work. When your child can't breathe, you grasp at anything. Then, one afternoon, a friend came to our Connecticut farm and told us of a famous doctor who had gotten results in allergy cases with a high protein diet.

"Why don't you drop in and see him?" she said. "Tell him I sent you. It can't do any harm."

This doctor's theory was that man is harmed by his own blundering treatment of natural foods. Our bodies are often starved for lack of right food values, such as are found in stone-ground whole-wheat flour. I went home and boldly announced that I was going to buy some real whole-wheat, and bake my son a loaf of bread.

Now I'd never made bread in my life, but in the kitchen I struggled to reproduce an old-fashioned home-made loaf. All the old cookbook recipes had a long list of ingredients: whole-wheat flour (stone ground); pure honey; fresh, whole dairy milk; pure butter; and so forth. "Nobody makes bread with these anymore," I said to myself. But I decided to use them all.

The noise of clanging utensils that followed must have sounded like a battery of bakers at work. Not knowing what I was doing, I made a dough, and stuck it in the oven. An hour later I took out my first loaf of bread.

It was awful.

On the outside it was crooked; it sunk low in the middle and was about as solid as a brick. When I put it on the table, I could see my family choke. It took weeks of repeated trial and error— still not knowing what I was doing—before at last I produced a loaf that caused Henry to sit back, his eyes bright, and say: "Now that's *bread*."

Slowly, with his new diet, my son's wheezing and coughing lessened, and the child grew stronger. I certainly do not want to say it was my home-baked bread that cured my son of asthma. There was another factor working: strange "coincidences" that I seemed to have no control over. The development of this first successful loaf into Pepperidge Farm bread was to come about through a chain of such unusual coincidences that I hesitate to use the word. Some people would call them "accidents." I like to think that God and prayer work through people in remarkable ways.

For instance, many friends, tasting my bread, began to suggest that I put it on the market. A few days later, I made eight loaves of bread and took them down to a local grocer.

"I would like you to taste a piece of bread," I said, happening upon a very successful sales technique. The grocer's face brightened. Three hours later he telephoned to tell me excitedly that the bread was already sold out and to ask for a regular supply.

Although I knew nothing of manufacturing, or marketing, of pricing, or of making bread in quantities, with that phone call Pepperidge Farm bread was born.

One evening Henry casually mentioned that he was helping a fund-raising campaign for the Visiting Nurses. He told me the story of Lillian Wald, a wealthy woman who was devoting her life to service for others through her nursing program.

"I'd love to meet this woman," I remarked, but, knowing how busy her life was, I never dreamed it would be possible. About a year later I was out for a drive when my car broke down, "accidentally." From a large house nearby a chauffeur appeared and personally did the repair work. He would accept nothing for his trouble.

"Surely there's some way I can thank you," I said.

"It was my employer sent me down, Ma'am. Miss Wald."

Taking the opportunity, I walked up to the house, rang the bell, and met Lillian Wald. We became close friends. It was she who inspired me to think of my bread-making as both an enterprise and a form of service to others.

Perhaps through such "coincidences" (our son's illness, inventing our bread recipe, friends suggesting making bread en masse, and now the meeting with Miss Wald), perhaps through these accidents, God broadens our backs to do work we never dream lies within our capabilities.

Certainly, the problems that arose seemed beyond my capabilities. First, as the demand for our bread increased, we had to get stone-ground flour in large quantities. Almost all the stone grinding mills had disappeared decades ago. We even considered setting up our own mill, but that would have required thousands of dollars and I was determined to let all new equipment come from profits. Yet there could be no profits without flour.

One day, by *chance*, we heard from an acquaintance this completely casual remark: "You know, there's a man up in Connecticut who has an interesting hobby. Has an old-fashioned stone mill. Grinds his own flour."

My husband and I rushed up to meet him and discovered a mill that had ground flour since Revolutionary days. I explained my project.

"You realize, of course, that my mill is just a hobby," the gentleman said. That was the trouble. None of us knew anything about milling; the art of the stone mill had been almost lost. We went ahead, though, using his flour, knowing we were doing many things wrong for lack of technical knowledge.

Somehow we expanded, moving our pots and pans from the kitchen to the stables. Then, one day a woman reporter was sent out to the farm to do a story on us. Later she called me at my office in the stable.

"Mrs. Rudkin, I'm down at an old second-hand book store. I just *happened* to run across a book you might be interested in."

It was an old, technical volume on stone milling. It turned out to be the bible of the trade—and had all the answers we needed to operate the old stone mill.

This last event drew my husband into the business. Henry had always taken my commercial bread-making somewhat as a joke. Now, through the technical side of the business, he became greatly interested.

"You know, our stones aren't far enough apart," he would say. "We've got to do something about that; it says here you can burn your wheat if the stones aren't properly set." Out came his calipers and measuring tapes.

Henry today is one of the outstanding milling experts in America. Bit by bit he began turning his full time away from Wall Street towards making bread.

Henry at first laughed at the way I kept books. He would walk into the stable, and see me scribbling on little scraps of paper. This was my bookkeeping: so much in, so much out; the rest was profit.

Now his attitude changed. "Anyone who puts out a thousand loaves of bread a day is in business, Peg. Let's set up a regular bookkeeping system so you'll know where you stand."

A thousand loaves of bread a day. Then 4,000 . . . 10,000. We moved from the stables to an abandoned gas station. Then we had to build a new plant, specially designed for hand-kneaded bread.

As we increased production, we were, of course, faced with difficulties keeping the home-made quality. Yet we've done it. When I was invited to give a lecture before a group of manufacturers, I said, "We succeeded at Pepperidge Farm by breaking all the rules of manufacturing." We have kept each of the theories of bread-making we started with in the kitchen of our farmhouse.

This means extra help, no rigid standardizations, and family relationship with every employee.

Years after I rattled and clanged my way through that first loaf of bread, we are producing thousands of loaves a day: whole-wheat and white. We have three bakeries, four mills, over one hundred employees. Our bread has been eaten, literally, half the world over.

If, as I worked over that first soggy loaf, I had seen the modern bakery, I would have said, "That's impossible. It belongs to someone else." I didn't realize that you walk a mile by taking one step at a time.

Grandmother's first words to me, "Don't be afraid to step out," have come to a fuller meaning. We know now, not to be afraid to get started on some new venture just because the end of the mile seems so far away. We don't worry about the *end* of the mile—we just take the first step. God will broaden the back to bear the burden. *March 1952*

TRUTH—IT'S GOOD BUSINESS
BY DAVID SCHWARTZ

Rent-A-Wreck

For the past 16 years I have bought and sold more than 3,000 used cars. And now I rent them. Through it all I believe I have learned a secret of business success.

It's not really a secret, though I don't think enough people take advantage of it.

Part of it lies in the fact that I am lazy.

Let me explain how it all happened.

In 1968 I began working my way through the University of California at Los Angeles. A friend who was buying a new car offered to sell me his old one for the same price the dealer was allowing as a trade-in. I bought it, then resold it, making a $200 profit.

It seemed a good way to help defray school expenses, and from then on I bought and sold cars in this manner. By the time I graduated I found myself in the used-car business.

I began with a few old cars on a small lot on West Pico Boulevard in West Los Angeles. Here I really put into practice what I had learned in my college car dealings. If something was wrong with a car I was selling, I'd try to fix it. If I couldn't fix it, I would tell the prospect up front. If the battery was weak, he'd know. If the car used a lot of oil, he wouldn't have to drive a hundred miles to find out.

"Dave, you're nuts," argued a friend. "Everybody knows you can't make any money in the used-car business that way."

This is where my being lazy came in.

The last thing I wanted was an angry customer charging back with fire in his eyes about some unexpected thing going wrong with his car. For me, this would be too much work and aggravation.

So if a fellow came onto the lot and said, "Look, I have $500 to spend on a car, what have you got?" I'd ask him what he needed.

"Oh, something with four doors."

"Well, here's a 1965 Ford Sedan that runs pretty well. But after you drive it a hundred miles or so the transmission will slip a little."

He takes it out on a test drive, comes back and says, "O.K., Dave, it's a deal."

He leaves happy, and I'm happy. He knows what he's getting, and I have made a little profit. That's equitable; good news for everybody.

That first year I lost money, really took a bath. But it wasn't my car-selling tactics. I hadn't yet learned how to judge people. Folks would give me money down on a car with a promise to pay. Sometimes their word wasn't good. Eventually I was able to tell the people I could trust and the ones I couldn't. I guess you'd call that discernment.

My business began to grow like gangbusters. Satisfied customers told others, "Hey, if you want a good deal on a used car, see Dave Schwartz." Soon my little lot was jammed bumper to bumper with cars.

Then, through ignorance, I stepped into another good thing. The man across the street on Pico Boulevard was fighting a losing battle with his big car lot and some store buildings. He had sunk himself too deep with other investments and owed his mother-in-law plus a third trustee on the property.

He wanted someone to put down $4,000 and take over the payments. Again, wise business heads warned me, "Dave, his overall asking price is way too much; the property isn't worth it."

Well, I figured I could make the payments and I did need the space badly. All I needed was the down payment. And this is where I learned another lesson.

Basically, I'm a simple, informal guy who feels at home in blue jeans, a sweater, old tennis shoes and a baseball cap. However, when I went to the bank to borrow the down payment, I thought I'd improve my image. So I put on a three-piece suit, slicked down my hair and donned tight, shiny shoes. Well, during the interview with the bank loan officer, I felt as if I were suffocating. My hands were sweaty and I was restless. The banker sensed this, of course, and had absolutely no confidence in me.

A few weeks later, I went to another bank in my normal clothes—jeans, old shoes—feeling perfectly at home and confident. I got the loan.

I bought the property on Pico Boulevard and moved my car business across the street, calling it Bundy Used Cars, because it was close to the better-known Bundy Boulevard. (Today, the property is worth many times what I paid for it.)

More and more customers came in. Most of my cars were clunkers, but they all ran. Still, people would walk by and laugh, asking, "How do you have the nerve to sell such homely cars?"

I scratched my head and thought. They were right. So I asked a sign painter to make a new sign: BUNDY VERY USED CARS.

Then something happened that changed the whole course of my business.

A young woman walked in one morning carrying suitcases. "You know," she said, looking around our lot wonderingly, "ten different people told me to come here."

I was amazed; I could never have paid for that kind of advertising. It turned out she had just graduated from Harvard and had come to Los Angeles on a three-month work assignment. After looking over our stock, she bought a Corvair, "as is," for $100.

That afternoon she phoned wanting to know if I knew of a good mechanic in her area.

"No," I said. "Why?"

"Well, my car broke down."

"I'm sorry," I said. "I'll have it towed in. But come on over and I'll give you your money back."

She almost dropped the phone.

Later, on our lot, she found another car she liked. "Look," she suggested, "instead of my buying it, how about renting it to me for the three months I'll need it? I'll be glad to pay you $225."

"I'd like to," I said, "but I don't have the kind of insurance needed to rent cars."

"Well," she said thoughtfully, "how about selling me the car for $225 so you can put it in my name. I'll assume responsibility for insurance and then in three months I'll return the car to you free and clear."

I did some quick calculating. The car was really worth $400, but . . . if she was going to bring it back?

"O.K.," I said, "you've got a deal."

Three months later she drove up in the car, handed me the keys and kissed me. "God bless you, Dave," she said, "that was the best deal I've ever had!"

She waved good-bye and as I stood there holding the keys, I reflected on what had happened. I had the car, the money and a customer who seemed to be very happy. A light bulb lit up in my head.

I went to some other local lots that were renting cars. Every owner warned me away from it. "It's a can of worms, Dave, don't go near it." Most of them were pulling out of it.

I spent the next several weeks asking them why it wouldn't work. From what they told me I began to learn what they were doing wrong. So I began my own operation: Bundy Rent-A-Used-Car.

I have to admit my cars looked, well, very used. But I believed that the worse a car looked, the better it should run. So maybe the '63 Chevy had rusted fenders and a mismatched paint job, but we made sure everything mechanical was in apple-pie order before a customer drove it out.

But they sure looked awful.

As one couple drove out in a 1969 Mustang, I overheard his wife ask, "Where's the ashtray?"

"Honey," replied the husband, "the whole car is an ashtray."

A friend, Jeffrey Kramer, kidded me. "Dave, your cars are so old that their radios only get Tokyo Rose." He slapped his leg and laughed. "You ought to call this place Rent-A-Wreck."

Again that light bulb came on.

"I'll do it," I said.

"Do what?" he asked.

"Just wait and see."

I called my sign-painter friend, and that's how Rent-A-Wreck came into being.

There was a method in what my friend Jeffrey called my madness. I felt it steered away people who were too apprehensive, who would give me a lot of grief. I wanted only those folks who understood what they were getting, a car that was mechanically sound and safe but one that wouldn't necessarily bring admiring glances on Wilshire Boulevard.

Even to this day I hesitate renting to someone that I feel is going to be a complainer no matter how well he is treated. As I said, I'm basically lazy. I don't like to do anything over the second time. I'd rather take a little extra time at first to make sure it's done right. I believe every business transaction must be equitable, and that means people leaving with a smile, even if they're not customers. One would-be patron came into our office the other evening and after a few comments from him about our cars, I could smell trouble. I knew he'd never be satisfied. I couldn't just say "No, we won't rent to you." Instead I have developed a theory that works out well in practice. I call it finesse versus force.

So I said, "Look, I think you'll be much happier with Avis, where I know you'll find exactly what you want. I'll be happy to drive you over there."

I did just that and again there were two happy people—a pleased car renter, and a relieved me.

Our way of doing business became so successful that people in other parts of the country asked if we could franchise them.

Today, some 400 Rent-A-Wreck agencies cover the United States and Australia. We are one of the largest car-rental firms in the world.

Most of the people who drive Rent-A-Wrecks are doing it on their own nickel instead of expense accounts. They figure they drive a used car at home, so why not do the same when traveling and save as much as $100 a week. Today, our cars are only slightly more used than the "major" firms. In fact, we now offer new cars too. And all of them have been safety checked, run great and now come complete with ashtrays.

But there is one thing I stress to a prospective franchise. "If money is your only goal, then forget it." I believe that, in any enterprise, if you make money your god, then the business will never be really successful. For then you're never satisfied; you've put the cart before the horse.

But if a person enjoys filling needs and making people happy, then there's no end to his or her success and there's no need to worry about money. It was all put into one sentence 2,000 years ago by Jesus Christ when He said: "In everything do to others what you would have them do to you" (Matthew 7:12 NIV).

It's a very good principle for businesspersons too.

January 1985

THE REAL NUMBER ONE

BY DONALD SEIBERT

J. C. Penney

Last year I retired from my position as chairman of the board of the J. C. Penney Company. I had joined the firm as a shoe clerk in 1947, and I gradually made my way from assistant store manager to manager and on up the ladder. I loved retailing and I like to think it was the right career for me. And yet, there was a time when my life could have gone in an entirely different direction. It was also a time in which I learned something that would have stood me in good stead no matter what job I undertook.

Today, whenever I hear the limpid notes of a saxophone, my memory takes me back 38 years, and I can see myself, a member of a small dance band, fingering the yellowed keys of an oaken upright in an old pavilion on the shore of a lovely lake. That summer of 1946 was a time of transition for me. Like most young men of that day I was trying to pick up the pieces of my life after World War II. I was married and trying to decide whether to continue in engineering college or what. Before the war I'd had after-school jobs selling shoes, something I always enjoyed, and then there was my real burning interest, music. No matter what I chose to try for, desperate financial need and a new baby daughter made it urgent that I get started in *something*.

In May of 1946 I was offered a summer job playing the piano in an eight-piece orchestra at a resort on Chautauqua Lake in western New York State.

This could be the answer, I thought: *my entree into a real career.* Verna and I excitedly packed our suitcases and, with our little Donna, only six weeks old, we took a bus to Bemus Point where we joined other band members. Three saxophones, a trumpet, a trombone, a bass, a drummer, along with the band's manager. I was to be the pianist and vocalist.

For living quarters, we leased through Labor Day four rooms over a restaurant near the pavilion. Verna, the baby and I lived in one; another married musician and his family occupied the other; and the rest of the band, all bachelors, took the other two. Our landlord, a pleasant middle-aged man, helped support his family by renting out adjacent tourist cabins.

The summer began beautifully. The pavilion was a rambling white-frame building with boat docks for patrons who came to listen to "The Rhythmaires," with "The Romantic Vocals of Donny Seibert."

Things went well through June and part of July, but in mid-season, a windstorm churned the lake waters bringing a cold rain. "A freak summer storm," said the pavilion owner.

A few days later another "freak storm" hit with whitecaps heaving empty boat docks. A dismal rain dragged into the kind of sustained chilly gray weather that sends vacationers morosely heading home.

"Can't last," said our landlord, worry furrowing his brow as he surveyed empty restaurant tables and darkened cabins.

But it did. The late summer settled into a pattern of perverse weather. Too often I found myself singing about "the wind and the rain in your hair" to just a few people who undoubtedly didn't find the lyrics that romantic.

One night, while we were in the middle of "Deep Purple," I saw our manager talking anxiously with the pavilion owner, who gestured helplessly. Later our manager gave us the bad news. "He can't pay us right now . . . says he'll make it up soon as the weather breaks."

Our landlord listened sympathetically to our problem and said we could pay him when things got better.

Things got worse.

One morning we awakened to find that our manager had quietly disappeared. Now everyone started looking at everyone else out of the corner of his eye. We struggled on, but the gray mist scudding across the lake was as dark as the look on our landlord's face.

Not many days later, we awakened to find the rest of the band gone. Verna and I looked at each other with eyes full of questions.

"What . . . what do you think we should do, Don?" Verna asked in a husky voice.

I couldn't answer at the moment.

No one could blame the others for leaving after not being paid for two weeks. It would be simple for us to leave, too.

"After all," one member had muttered, "who can get blood out of a turnip?"

"You've got to look out for Number One," nodded another.

He was right, I thought. *I have to look out for number One.*

And then the moment of revelation.

Who *was* Number One?

As Verna and I stood there, I knew deep down there was only one answer: the God Who had sustained us, Who had helped Verna through a dangerous childbirth, Who had given us our little girl. *He* was Number One; the One Who directed us to love our neighbor as ourselves (Matthew 22:39).

Morning had dawned unnaturally bright that day as the sun, for a change, pushed through scattered clouds. I stepped outside into the fresh, forest-scented air. As I rounded the corner of the restaurant, I met our landlord. He stared at me in surprise.

"You? You didn't leave?"

"No," I shook my head. "No, we're staying on to the end of our lease."

Now he looked confused.

"About the rent," I said, stammering, "Uh, we can't pay in cash, but I was hoping maybe you'd have some work I can do for you here . . ."

"Oh, sure, sure," he brightened, "we'll find something."

A heavy load seemed to have slid off his shoulders.

From then on instead of playing piano and singing "Stardust," I cleaned tourist cabins, changed beds and washed sheets. With our landlord's permission I rented out the three other rooms whenever possible.

But that didn't happen often as the weather worsened. By the time Labor Day came, we still owed $150.

On checking around, I found that a grape-juice processing plant in Westfield paid 75 cents an hour. It was 20 miles away. But if I arose at 4:30 a.m., I could hike to the highway where a company truck picked up me and other itinerant workers.

It was rough work, hauling the heavy blanketlike canvas filters from the presses and washing them for the next processing. The temperature could go as high as 130 degrees, and my fingers cracked from the acid in the juice, but I worked with an enthusiasm I'd never had before.

Finally, in early October, I was able to pay up the last of our lease. Our landlord seemed deeply moved when we came in with the final rent. "It's not the money," he said as he thanked us. "It's just so reassuring to know that there are people in the world who are as good as their word." Then he added, "You'll go far, son, you'll go far."

By then, for me, it wasn't so much a matter of how *far* I'd go as *how* I'd get there, and I knew that so long as I looked out for the *real* Number One, I'd be doing it right.

Not long after that I got my job as a shoe clerk with J. C. Penney in Bradford, Pennsylvania. *May 1984*

THEY SAID I DIDN'T HAVE A PRAYER
BY GEORGE SHINN
Business College President

The five men seated at the conference table looked at one another. Then they looked at me. No one said a word, but I could read their minds, and what I read there made my heart sink.

I had used my last funds to hire these men, all experts in business management, to advise me on how to resolve the financial difficulties I was facing. For two hours we had been going over my books and records. They had asked searching questions, and I had attempted to answer them honestly.

Finally one of the lawyers—three of the men were lawyers and two were certified public accountants—cleared his throat. "George," he said, "would you mind stepping outside for a few minutes? We'd like to discuss all aspects of your situation frankly among ourselves."

Feeling like a condemned man, I waited outside. The minutes passed slowly. Finally the door opened and I was asked to rejoin the group. The lawyer spoke again. "I'm sorry to tell you this, George, but we can see only one solution for you. We feel you should give up and close your business schools." Give up! Here I was at age 28 with my own business—and now I was facing bankruptcy.

One of the lawyers accompanied me to the elevator. I guess he meant to be kind, but his parting words went through me like a knife. "George," he said, "why don't you go to work for someone else? You don't have a prayer, not a prayer!"

I went out of the building like a man in a daze. Give up. That was all the experts could suggest. Well, I thought with sudden grim determination, I wasn't going to take that way out. There had to be a better way, there had to be. But still I could hear that lawyer's voice with its mocking echoes: "You haven't got a prayer, not a prayer!"

The whole thing had come as such a shock that it almost seemed unreal. In the first place, I never expected to have a business of my own. When I finished high school in Kannapolis, North Carolina, my goal was to make $100 a week and to buy a new car every three or four years.

My first full-time job was as an unskilled laborer in a factory. After a couple of years I developed trouble with my back. X rays showed an injury to my spine, probably from playing football in high school. The doctor told me I could do no more heavy work.

My mother recommended college.

I knew I needed more education, but there wasn't any money for it. My father had died when I was eight, leaving a lot of debts, and my mother had gone to work, sometimes holding down two jobs at once, to keep us going.

College seemed out of the question, but in nearby Concord was a small business college. I registered there for a two-year course.

Six months later, my savings ran out. I asked the school manager if there was any way I could earn my tuition, and he took me on as the school's janitor. For pocket money, I found a part-time job in a bakery.

One Saturday morning, I had just finished my janitorial chores and changed into my street clothes when two high-school girls came in. One of them asked, "Do you work here?"

"Yes," I said. But I didn't tell them the distinguished position that I held!

She said, "We're thinking of going to college after we finish high school. Can you tell us something about this school?"

That was easy. I liked the school. I felt I was learning important things about business administration, and I knew the school was providing a valuable community service in training young people who still were too inexperienced to get a good job in business. As I gave the girls a tour of the rooms I had just cleaned, I also told them what a great school it was. Before they left, they enrolled for the fall semester.

Monday morning, when I gave the applications to the school director, he was delighted. "George," he said, "in addition to your job as janitor, if you want to do some recruiting for the school, I'll pay you ten dollars for each student you bring in."

When you believe in something and are enthusiastic about it, you can't help but be successful. Eventually I was earning enough from recruiting to quit the bakery job. Then, when I finished the two-year course myself, the director hired me as a full-time recruiter.

I really enjoyed my work. I looked upon recruiting as more than a job. Not only was I helping the school, but I was also helping young people to improve themselves and their futures. Even so, I wasn't satisfied. I wanted to become more involved in the school and feel more like a part of it. I was looking for a future myself.

One day I asked one of the owners if there was any chance that I might buy into the school as a partner. To my surprise, he said yes. We agreed on the price and that he would make deductions in my salary each week until I paid him off.

They owned three other business colleges in the state. I visited those and met the staff members and liked them. Soon I heard that the owners were ready to get out of the school business and move into other fields. With an audacity that was beyond my years and experience, I offered to buy them out.

After I took over, I soon discovered I was facing trouble. There were unpaid bills totaling thousands of dollars. On the horizon were creditors with their lawyers. Some staff members hadn't been paid for weeks, some for months. Properties were mortgaged to the hilt. I tried to get a loan at practically every bank in North Carolina, but my applications were rejected. I didn't know any people I could borrow money from. That was when I decided to have a meeting with the lawyers and accountants.

For days the words I had heard there haunted me: *not a prayer, not a prayer, not a prayer.* Then late one day, as I was driving home, deep in despair, I suddenly realized, "But I do have a prayer! It's all I have left." As a small boy I had been active in the church, but when I became a little older I drifted away from it all. My faith had not diminished; I just hadn't called upon it lately.

I stopped the car along the road, and I let the words pour out of me: "Lord, You know what a mess I'm in. Everybody says I'm sunk. I don't believe You feel that way. Help me, Lord. I'm turning the company over to You. You do the guiding and I'll do the work. And anything that comes to me, Lord, I'll share with You."

A sense of great relief shot through me. I felt as though I had just been lifted out of a nightmare. I still had my problems and I still had no money. But even so, it seemed that a huge burden had been lifted.

That night I had my first good sleep in weeks. When I awoke in the morning, I felt so exhilarated that I bounded out of bed and said aloud, "Good morning, Lord!"

When I got to the office, the secretary was on the phone. She placed a hand over the mouthpiece and whispered, "It's that text-book publisher in New York. He's having a fit."

"I'll talk to him," I said. She was surprised. For weeks I had been dodging creditors on the phone and not even reading their threatening letters. I took the phone, "Good morning, Mr. Johnson," I said. "I hope you're in good health."

"Not financially," he said. "Mr. Shinn, what are you going to do about this bill of yours?"

"I'm going to pay it," I said. "In fact, I'll send you a check today. I don't know how much, but I'll send you something."

"Good," he said. "I look forward to it."

I didn't even have to open the checkbook to know that the most I could send him was one dollar, so I sent a check for that amount. A few days later, he called again and said, "Mr. Shinn, I got your check this morning. It's only for one dollar. Did you make a mistake?"

"No, I didn't," I said.

"Then are you trying to be cute?"

"I've never been more serious," I said. "I'm going to pay that bill, but you'll have to let me do it in weekly amounts I can afford. Will you go along with that?"

He thought about it, then said, "For the time being."

The next week, I was able to send him seven dollars. Gradually the bill was paid off. So were other bills, as creditors agreed to give us more time.

At first, I didn't want to tell others about my experience with the Lord on the highway, fearing that they would think I had gone off the deep end. But then I figured that if the Lord was guiding me He was probably guiding others on our team, and I decided it would be a good idea if they knew about it.

At a staff conference one morning, I said, "I think we ought to open this meeting with a prayer." Puzzled looks went around the table, followed by bowed heads. Knowing that I was going to have trouble with my first public prayer, I had written it out beforehand. And then I told them what had happened to me.

This was the turn in the road for us, as a company and as individuals, a turn to the Lord. And the answers started coming, sometimes even popping into my mind in the middle of the night. We began to reorganize the schools, expanding curriculums, increasing facilities and trying new ideas, such as offering valuable programs for veterans returning from Vietnam. We did our best to offer first-class training in many business skills at moderate tuition costs, preparing students for successful careers in the business world.

Enrollment grew to over 5,000 students; new schools were added to our chain of colleges. As our expertise increased, other schools throughout the country started coming to us for consultation services. Today the once nearly bankrupt organization has a staff of over 800, and serves as a management consultant to colleges in over 28 states.

When I look back through the years, I'm amazed by the difference that simply turning to God and letting him direct things has made for me. Every morning when I wake up and get out of bed, I still say, "Good morning, Lord!" because, thanks to Him, that's just what it is.   *January 1977*

MY OWN CUP OF TEA

BY MO SIEGEL

Celestial Seasonings

I am a teamaker.

I'm the president of a company called Celestial Seasonings; we produce and sell our own herb teas. You may have seen a box of our tea on a grocery store shelf; if you have, then you've probably noticed that we have a unique way of decorating it. You may see a drawing of the Sleepytime bear in his nightcap, or some picnickers beneath a blossoming orange tree, or an ancient Chinese emperor. And we put lots of wise quotations on our boxes, too, such as:

One of the most difficult things to give away is kindness—it is usually returned.   —Court R. Flint

Usually, when people see our boxes for the first time, they ask us, Why? Why the art and why the quotes? Unwittingly, perhaps, they're asking me to tell them the story of Mo Siegel. For to understand why a box of our tea looks the way it does, you have to understand the teamaker. And you can understand the teamaker by reading the quotes on his boxes.

A man is not a man when he is created; he is only begun. His manhood must come with years. —Henry Ward Beecher

At the age of six, I knew I would be a businessman. In fact, as a child, I had my own business in our small Colorado mountain town, picking wild berries and selling them to ladies for jams and jellies. It put a few dollars in the pocket, to be sure, but most of all, it let me be outdoors with the plants and mountains I loved so much. I figured I could live my life there.

When I was 15, I went away to a Catholic prep school. I'm not sure why I was enrolled there—we weren't Catholic; we weren't even Christian. I think my dad figured that the school might get me out of the outdoors and inside for a little book-learning.

He was right, too. And do you know what book I began to do my learning from? The New Testament. It fascinated me; I began reading the Gospels, then the letters of Paul. And, with my interest sparked, I went on to other spiritual writings. I remember especially the Frenchman, Teilhard de Chardin, who wrote about getting along with others, doing things for them, about a universal community based on Christ's love for us. I remember praying, too—I'd never done that before. I left that school forever changed, touched by a Father in Heaven.

But I also left with a feeling of "Now what?" That fall I enrolled at a small Colorado college—for two months. I hated it, being cooped up in classes with my nose forced into a book. I didn't have four years to become formally educated. Education would have to be self-taught. Life was calling, opportunities waiting. I just wanted to be myself, to love God and to serve others. But how do you live on ideals?

Why should we be in such desperate haste to succeed, and in such desperate enterprises? If a man does not keep peace with his companions, perhaps it is because he hears a different drummer. Let him step to the music which he hears, however measured or far away. —Henry David Thoreau

Different?—that was me all right. I was the long-haired guy with the peace symbols sewn on tattered blue jeans. I longed for my independence, the chance to serve God, to do what I wanted to do instead of attending college. It was a tough road; I invested and lost my few saved dollars. I lived in Aspen, Colorado, surrounded by the mountains and woods. I co-owned a health-food store but didn't make enough to eat and pay the rent. Then, restless and broke, I went southeast and worked on a fishing trawler off the Florida coast. And back to Boulder, Colorado, carrying a sandwich board for advertising. But these jobs were just jobs, money to live on. They were other people's ideals, other people's dreams. Someday I was going to discover what I could do myself! I was reborn of the Spirit, and with Jesus in my life, I desired to serve others by selling useful products.

Ironically, the idea came as I wandered through some mountain fields one day, fields thick with different herbs and flowers. I knew, loved and studied the plants in the mountains: spearmint, with its fragrant green leaves; chamomile, with its small, daisy-like heads; blackberry leaves; rosehips. They reminded me of the health-food store back in Aspen. The store sold a peppermint herb tea; it was all the rage. I was convinced that herb teas were good for you. I hoped to make a much better-tasting cup of tea than those currently on the market. What would happen, for example, if different herbs were mixed so they'd complement each other?

I started gathering all kinds of herbs in big burlap sacks. I'd tote them home and then brew up different blends into a cup of tea. Some tasted pretty good, others pretty horrible. But one day ... "This is it, this is it!" I yelled. I called the concoction "Mo's 36" because there were 36 different herbs in it. That was the beginning of a company called Celestial Seasonings. I was 20 years old.

Without a worthy follower, a worthy dream vanishes.
—Charles Edwards

What was so worthy about a tea company? I was making a good, beneficial product. And, it was mine. I could give customers the kind of tea they wanted. I could even decorate the boxes the way the frustrated artist in me wanted. I guess you could say that that teabag was my own cup of tea.

A friend of mine, John Hay, teamed up with me to sell Mo's 36 in the health-food stores around Boulder. I also teamed up

80

with another important person—I got married to Peggy. Now we began working in earnest! We cut the herbs and blended them. Peggy hand-sewed our teabags.

So one summer afternoon, armed with some cases of Mo's 36, Peggy and I climbed into our old, dilapidated Datsun and headed toward New York. At most of the towns along the way, we'd stop and I'd head into the local store with a case of tea. "This will be the biggest herb tea company in America in three years," I'd enthusiastically tell the store owners. "Do you want to start with us now?" And he'd look at me, and then at the cloth tea packages sporting bright colors and inspirational phrases, and usually laugh me right out of the store. A few people tried the tea, and agreed to stock it. Later, back in Boulder, John and I kept trying out new blends with new tastes and new names—Red Zinger, Orange Spice. Finally our perseverance paid off—a large food distributor agreed to carry our line. We rented a building, hired salesmen, delivery people.

Peggy hand-sewed 10,000 muslin bags needed for our first shipment, and that year we sold $14,000 worth of tea. Each year after that, the company grew.

One thing we wanted to do was stop importing one of our ingredients: peppermint. But the American crop was all being taken by the chewing-gum people for peppermint oil. So in 1974, we bought a field of the best peppermint in the country, while it was all still in the ground. And when harvest time came, we took half of our staff to Wisconsin to harvest it. But day after day, for two weeks, it rained. Then the frost hit. We were left with a nearly unusable field of peppermint and a bill for it that suddenly threatened to sink the company.

I didn't know what we were going to do. There wasn't enough money to pay that peppermint bill and our employees.

Do you know what kept us going? Our employees. They said they believed in the company, and would work the next week even if we couldn't pay them. Slowly we pulled ourselves back up.

The highest reward for a man's toil is not what he gets for it, but what he becomes by it.   —John Ruskin

Once the business got back on its feet, we began to hire new managers to do the financial planning, the advertising—we even hired a Ph.D. in nutrition to do the tea testing. And Mo Siegel began getting accolades for building a successful company out of nothing.

Maybe that's why I kept trying to run the company as if I was the only one who could think. It wasn't uncommon at all to see me race into someone's office, ask to know what he was working on, give my suggestions and corrections, and then do the same thing in someone else's office. I convinced myself that I was doing them all a favor by helping out like that.

My managers disagreed. "Mo, you've got to let us do our jobs," one of them said, looking me in the eye. "Back off a little. Be less of an entrepreneur. Your company's grown up now . . ."

I didn't know what to do or say, except what I always do when I'm faced with a tough problem in the business—try to figure out what God would have me do. This one was the toughest of all, because the problem was me. But the answer came clearly enough. "For what will it profit a man, if he gains the whole world and forfeits his life" (Matthew 16:26 RSV). So did the meaning: that all the money I made in tea wasn't worth a dime if I couldn't make any friends in doing it. Helping others didn't mean just offering customers a good, healthy tea, it means showing co-workers more respect, and not taking myself so seriously.

You cannot build character and courage by taking away man's initiative and independence.   —Abraham Lincoln

Once, when we were stymied by a production problem, someone said, "Why don't you ask the line workers themselves?" So we did, realizing no one would know better about how to improve efficiency on a production line than the people who work there.

All of our employees are now part of work teams composed of people from several different levels of the company. Quality is up, costs down, mostly because of teamwork and workers' suggestions. And through ideas like profit sharing, they're not just helping the company; they're helping themselves.

When you look through plain glass, you see people, but if you cover it with silver, you stop seeing others and see only yourself.   —ancient proverb

That first batch of 10,000 hand-sewn tea bags has grown to more than three-quarters of a billion tea bags a year. It's always tempting to think that yes, I have finally made it. But it's just when I start admiring myself in that silver-covered glass that something comes along to remind me how far I have yet to go. One year, it was iced tea.

In this country, 75 percent of all the tea consumed is iced. Yet we'd barely touched that market, even though we make what I think is a good iced tea.

So our advertising people spent a lot of time figuring out the best way to present the product. They drew up television and magazine ads comparing our tea to other products on the markets. We named our competitors, told how tests showed our tea was better.

But just days before the debut of the campaign was set, we scrapped it and went without any advertising at all.

What happened? When I was looking over the campaign, I started thinking about where our company had come from and where it was going. Becoming a big businessman didn't make me stop needing to be a worthy follower, of my dream, however different, and of God. And yet, here we were, trying to grow at someone else's expense. It wasn't right. I couldn't bring myself to make money bad-mouthing a rival tea company. And so I told our employees. "If it doesn't follow the Golden Rule, then I don't want to participate in it."

Celestial has come a long way. But I hope in the midst of increasing automation and sophisticated marketing practices, one thing has stayed the same: our commitment to run this business the way God would have us do it.

Can you really mix herbs and faith and big business successfully? I think the answer to that is on one of our boxes, too:

When love and skill work together, expect a masterpiece.

February 1984

HOW TO ADD BY SUBTRACTING
BY R. DAVID THOMAS
Wendy's International, Inc.

My table companion at a fund-raising dinner was complaining about how busy he was. "I really shouldn't be here tonight," he said, and then went on to tell me about all the demands made on his time.

"Why is life so . . . so cluttered?" he sighed deeply, not really expecting an answer.

"Maybe it's because we allow it to be," I replied with a sympathetic smile.

There was a time when I'd constantly let my own life get too cluttered. But a number of years ago, I stumbled on a good antidote for an overly complicated existence. Oddly enough, the answer came out of a business crisis, but I've been able to apply it to my personal life as well.

It happened in the winter of 1962. I was 29 then, with a wife and four children. I was about to stake our futures, my job—everything—on a risky business venture.

I was working for a restaurant chain in Fort Wayne, Indiana. Four units that my boss had an interest in were in Columbus, Ohio, and they were in deep, deep trouble. My boss had even tried to sell them, but nobody was interested.

Something told me I could do something with them. Maybe I was being presumptuous, but by then I already had 17 years of experience in the food business. I'd begun working in restaurants at the age of 12 in Knoxville, Tennessee, as a counterman. In the Army I ran two mess halls and a bakery. After my hitch, I took a job with the restaurant chain, but in spite of a fancy title, I was earning only a modest salary. I was ambitious and full of ideas. Now, with this crisis in Columbus, I had a gut feeling that this could be my golden opportunity.

My boss supported me by saying that the stores could be turned around if someone would dedicate himself to doing it.

In early January, I went to Columbus to assess the situation. Business was bad; the management was worse. But there was one man who popped in there from time to time whom I really liked, a man I had known for a number of years. He was a colorful character from Kentucky who had an unusual recipe he'd created for fried chicken. His name was Harland Sanders and everybody called him the Colonel.

The Colonel had worked hard for many years, traveling around, selling franchises for his fried chicken to restaurants. He had a stake in our four failing restaurants. Whenever I'd see him out in the kitchen, fuming and fussing over his special chicken gravy, I'd feel sorry for him. He was owed a lot of money, and if the restaurants failed, he'd be sure to lose it.

But even my friend the Colonel didn't want me in Columbus.

"Dave, don't be a fool!" he thundered into the phone when I called him after returning to Fort Wayne. "Now you can uproot that wife and those kiddies of yours if you've a mind to, but I'm tellin' you as a friend that things are just too far gone here! Listen to the Colonel, boy, and don't come!"

I weighed the pros and cons, I spent a long time praying about it, and finally I decided to go. At the end of June, we packed our belongings and moved to Columbus.

I started off by reorganizing the staffs of all four restaurants. There was little money for the day-to-day operation; our credit was zero. We owed everybody. Even the Colonel was obliged to make the deliveries of his secret blend of herbs and spices C.O.D. Who could blame him? He didn't want to lose any more money.

I worked hard day and night, but there was no real improvement. I *had* to find an answer—some way to turn things around. But what was it? I had the feeling it was right there, under our noses, but I couldn't get a handle on it.

At night I'd take the problem home with me, to plague my poor wife who was trying to get the new house organized. Pacing up and down beside half-empty packing crates, I'd say, "Honey, there's something I ought to be doing that I'm not . . ." And I'd throw up my hands and stomp out to the kitchen for coffee. I was sure of one thing: I was not going to give up.

So I continued to worry, rack my brain and pray. And did I pray! Not that I thought for one minute that the good Lord was going to dump a full-blown miracle in my lap. With God and me it had always been a 50-50 deal; me working my darn'dest and trying to obey the Ten Commandments seven days a week, and Him doing the rest. But nothing seemed to be happening.

I'd walk around those restaurants, hoping the answer would come leaping out of the woodwork. In the pantries I'd survey row upon row of pickles, soup, olives, catsup. *It can't be that we're not well-stocked*, I'd think. Our menus were fine; it took 10 minutes to read them. We offered everything from baked beans to the Colonel's fried chicken. *Plenty there to choose from . . .*

But then I'd look at the half-empty restaurant and parking lot . . .

Maybe advertising was the answer. But we didn't have money for that either. Nevertheless, I went down to a radio station in town and talked to the manager about some spot ads. When he began discussing rates, I cleared my throat and said, "Look . . . we're having a little cashflow problem right now. Do you think we could spread the payments out a bit?"

The man got the picture. I held my breath.

"I tell you what, Thomas," he said after a minute's reflection. "That fried chicken is the best thing you serve. I'll swap you some spots for some chicken."

"It's a deal!" I said, grabbing his hand and pumping it vigorously. Driving home I was in a good mood for the first time in days. Praise God, we were making progress!

Suddenly it hit me so hard I almost swerved off the road: *the Colonel's chicken!*

"That fried chicken is the best thing you serve," the man had said. It was true—everybody loved it.

Instead of driving home, I turned the car around and headed for one of the restaurants. Ten minutes later the cooks and crew were startled to see me come striding into the kitchen. I went straight to the pantry and jerked the pull-chain on the light. I stood in the open door, while the lamp swung, making crazy shadows on the walls. There they were: row upon row of pickles, olives, catsup, soup and everything else I'd been so proud of. Sure we had enough inventory—*we had too much!* I strode into the dining room and looked at the menu-board. Sure it was filled—*it was too crowded!* The darned thing read like a Sears-Roebuck catalog!

What we needed to do was simplify. We had to "accentuate the positive," and for us, the positive was Colonel Sanders' Kentucky Fried Chicken!

The more I thought about it, the more sense it made. If I sold all that expensive inventory, I'd have the cash I needed to buy chicken and the Colonel's herbs and spices. It was a way out of the financial bind. And if I limited my menu to chicken, salad, dessert and beverages, I'd be able to maintain high quality. It seemed so simple. I couldn't get over that, the simplicity. And yet it was in the simplicity that I was sure the strength of the idea lay.

Business picked up. In the weeks that followed, we changed our name to Colonel Sanders' Kentucky Fried Chicken Take-Home. We sold chicken in buckets and barrels with the Colonel's beaming face on them. And business continued to build until the day came when I was able to hand the Colonel a check for the entire amount of our debt to him. The old man's hand trembled and he cried. He obviously had never expected to see a penny of it, but I'd been sure I would pay him back. After all, you have to have morals in business—honesty and integrity are your most important assets. I've always believed that "your word's your bond."

So there it was, an unexpected answer to the problem in our restaurants—an answer that anybody can apply in business or in his or her personal life. Simplify. Clear the shelves. Thin out the daily menu to make room for the things that really matter. Turn off the TV; talk to one another. Instead of driving off in 10 different directions on the weekend, concentrate on a family project at home. Say no to the trivial; say yes to God.

Eventually, when I began a restaurant of my own, I kept that principle in mind. This time I wasn't going to offer a menu of only chicken. I'd give the public something I'd loved ever since I was a kid working behind a counter in Knoxville—hamburgers. But I'd still keep the menu simple. I'd have a little restaurant, I thought, with some Tiffany-style lamps and bentwood chairs to go with my old-fashioned hamburgers. And I'd name my place after my daughter. I'd call it Wendy's ...   *June 1982*

JUST PLAIN DAVE
BY R. DAVID THOMAS
Wendy's International, Inc.

It used to be the only time folks wanted my signature was when it was on the bottom of a check.

Things have changed. The other day while I was in New York waiting at a light to cross Fifth Avenue, a man with his little boy asked for my autograph.

"You Wendy's father?" piped up the little fellow, who recognized me from my television commercials.

"I sure am," I said as I signed one of the little postcards I carry picturing my redheaded daughter and me.

Being asked for my autograph is a new experience, and you know, I kind of enjoy it. But if someone had told me 20 years ago that people would someday stop me in the street for my signature, I would have said they were crazy. The fact is I never enjoyed the limelight. I was always the guy behind the scenes. But life holds many surprises, and sometimes the things that intimidate you most can turn out to be the biggest sources of strength.

It all started about a year and a half ago when our advertising agency was looking for new ideas to promote our company. I invited them to my office to help them learn more about my philosophy and how Wendy's operates. I guess I was so enthusiastic that they suggested I appear in commercials myself.

At first I thought they were kidding. After all, I'm just a grill man who got a couple of breaks along the way and made the most of them. In fact, if some kind people hadn't adopted me as a baby, I don't know where I'd be today. But even with their help, growing up was tough. I got my first job at 12 years old working at the counter of a Knoxville restaurant. You could say I learned the business from the counter up!

When I opened my first Wendy's in 1969, I never dreamed that years later we'd have 3,800 restaurants and annual sales of $3 billion. So I guess what I'm saying is that when the TV people asked me to appear in our commercials, I thought they had the wrong guy.

I knew I'd never match Wendy's best-known spokesperson, Clara Peller, the elderly lady who caught the nation's attention a few years ago by asking, "Where's the beef?" Despite her age, Clara was one spunky lady right up to her death two years ago. We miss her a lot.

Eventually the ad agency and Charlie Rath, our head of marketing, persuaded me to give in, and I reluctantly went to New York to make a commercial. And though I resolved to try my best, those first attempts were the hardest things I've ever done. The first thing they told me was, "Dave, just be yourself." But in front of those cameras, it was easier said than done. After 10 tries, they told me I needed more energy, "but just be yourself . . ." Then they told me I needed to talk faster, talk slower, look this way, look that way, but above all else, just be myself! Being myself was turning out to be harder than I thought—particularly when others were telling me how.

The worst was when I tried to pronounce *"Muchas Gracias!"* for our Taco Salad commercial. I couldn't get it right. I'd blurt, "Muchas gracy" or "Macho grassy." For four hours I stumbled again and again. Finally, on a break, I sat down wiping my brow.

But I kept on trying with that Taco Salad commercial and finally got it right. I also started to get something else right. While watching the TV crew adjust their lights, I kept thinking about working with Colonel Sanders on his radio spots 20 years ago. He was no great actor, just a gentleman who believed he had the greatest fried chicken to come down the pike. He was so enthusiastic about his product that he completely forgot himself in his sales pitch. He was a natural. And that was because he *was* just himself—not somebody else's idea of how he should be.

Well, I thought, *I certainly believe in what I'm doing too.* Feeding folks was the work God called me to do, and so that's partly why I went into the restaurant business. A lot of folks think I pulled myself up alone. But I wasn't alone. I had God by my side. As the

Bible tells us in Isaiah 64:8, ". . . we *are* the clay, and thou our potter; and we all *are* the work of thy hand" (KJV). To me that means we have to accept ourselves as we are and be grateful for the way He made us.

That's the way it was with our old friend, Clara Peller. She never put on airs. No matter where we traveled, visiting with celebrities or whomever, she was always herself. And that was her charm in reaching folks.

In doing the next commercial, I decided that come what may, I would forget *acting* like myself. I'd just *be* myself—plain old Dave Thomas, a guy used to getting his hands wrinkled in hot dishwater, a guy who feels more at home making hamburgers than doing commercials.

And you know, I *was* more relaxed, more natural. I also found myself more confident, and when you're confident, you become more spontaneous, more adaptable and able to speak boldly. I'm reminded of that Scripture verse: "For if the trumpet give an uncertain sound, who shall prepare himself to the battle?" (I Corinthians 14:8 KJV). But when you speak out confidently, folks listen.

I also remembered that Colonel Sanders achieved his confidence by focusing on the other guy. I realized I had been focusing on myself, and I was tongue-tied because I was self-conscious. In the commercials I began to get over that by focusing on Bill Hudson, my director, making eye contact with him, talking *to* him, trying to please him. Soon his face lit up and he walked over to clap me on the shoulder. "Dave, you're doing great! What happened?"

I laughed. "Just trying to sell *you* a hamburger," I said.

The more I relaxed, the more confident I became. In fact, I even began coming up with suggestions for the TV crew, until one of them finally put me in my place. "Please, Mr. Thomas, we don't cook hamburgers, you don't get creative."

As time went on, I began to enjoy doing commercials, especially the humorous ones. And soon the words just came out naturally. One spot had me traipsing around a crowded Wendy's and complaining to the camera, "Who do you have to know to find a seat around here?" In another commercial I balance on a ladder trying to adjust a sign while Wendy stands below giving me directions. "Move it a little to the right, Dad . . . no, more to the left . . . no, further right." Finally, I wearily look down at her: "Wendy, don't you have something *else* to do?"

Folks enjoy it when you poke a little fun at yourself. They sympathize with you, get into your corner. And it's a good way to relax, especially when speaking before a group. So whether you're addressing a business meeting, church function or your class, remember what I learned: Just be yourself, focus on the folks you're talking to and let your natural enthusiasm take over.

And I learned one other important lesson. When you do the thing you fear the most, God might well have a pleasant surprise for you.

He sure surprised me.   *February 1991*

A MAN WITH A VIEW

BY WILLIAM WACHTER

Alta Mira Hotel

My wife, Ferne, and I stood in front of the small, 30-room hotel that summer morning in 1954, so taken by its potential that we didn't see the drawbacks. The Alta Mira was already 100 years old and looked it, with its peeling beige stucco facade, its three acres of weeds, its too-steep driveway and limited parking. "Just think, Ferne," I said, "what this place will be like with a little work."

I said the words while looking out over the waterside village of Sausalito and farther out over San Francisco Bay. It was the view that grabbed my attention. If caution did creep into my thinking, it was my age. At 56 I should have been thinking about retirement, not about refurbishing some run-down old hotel.

But I took Ferne's elbow and steered her up the hotel's rickety steps, exclaiming about the terrace I would build here someday. My terrace would be attached to a first-class hotel, like the places I had known in my childhood. Known *about*, that is. When I was a youngster, my family rarely visited such establishments. My father was a glazier in Berlin; men who installed windows for a living didn't stay in fancy hotels.

Ferne and I picked our way through the lobby. I could tell why its owners were anxious to sell. The lobby was dark; tiny windows defied you to enjoy the view. From somewhere in the building came gurgling and knocking sounds as water struggled to negotiate ancient pipes. Few people wanted to stay in this bathroom-down-the-hall place.

90

"But we'd make a go of it, Ferne. We'd knock down the walls, open up the view. Thousands of people would stream up here. Thousands."

Whatever I decided to do, Ferne said, she was with me. We drove back to the Fairmont Hotel in San Francisco, where I was catering manager and where friends had told me about the Alta Mira. "The hotel's a bargain, Bill. With your experience, you could make something out of it."

Experience I had, all right; I'd earned it through turning my back on an old European tradition. In the ordinary course of things at the turn of the century when I was born, a dutiful son in Germany was supposed to follow his father into the family business. But as I grew up I dreamed of going into hotel management, where I could work with people instead of with a putty knife. My father slapped his trousers leg and looked away when he heard this news. But eventually he let me go. I completed a 15-year apprenticeship, beginning with the Adlon Hotel in Berlin, and in time managed every phase of some of the finest hotels in Europe and America.

Now at last I was about to put these decades of experience to work with a hotel of my own. Ferne and I and two partners bought the Alta Mira for $100,000. Already I was sketching plans for my terrace, where people could eat outdoors under umbrellas during the day and by candlelight at night.

But those dreams seemed unattainable. One of my partners died shortly after we acquired the hotel. I bought out his interest, and there went the money for the plumbing system. The occasional guest who struggled up the hill didn't appreciate being awakened at 4:00 A.M. by clanging pipes. "I wouldn't stay in this boiler shop another night if it were *you* paying *me* for the room!" one man said as he made his escape.

And in trying to keep the kitchen open we put our purchases on the cuff. One morning, I came into the dim lobby and was pleased to see six gentlemen waiting there. "Customers!" I whispered to Ferne as I stepped behind the front desk.

"Look again, Bill," Ferne said. "Those are our suppliers wanting their money." Day after day the same purveyors waited in the lobby, bills in hand. We paid what we could.

After a year of limping along like this my other partner wanted out. With the very last of our resources we bought the final interest. The place was ours now, but what good was that? More months passed with less and less money for cleaning up the grounds and upgrading the kitchen. We had exhausted our funds and the patience of our creditors.

"Ferne, my dear, there is no hope left," I said one night in the fall of 1958, after four years of struggle. "You might as well pack our things."

Ferne agreed. I went down to the front desk from our apartment in the hotel to close the accounts of our two guests. Now and then I stopped to doodle on the plans for the terrace that would never come to pass. At eleven o'clock I decided to take a walk—the last ever as a hotel owner.

In the dark I headed up the path toward the rear of the grounds. Then, as I was ambling along, someone began speaking to me. The quiet voice seemed to come from inside the bushes. I looked, but couldn't see a soul, so I started walking again.

There. Again! I made out the words now: "If you follow me, I can help."

Who would be out this late, and why wasn't he showing his face? "Who's there?" I whispered. Then, more loudly, "Show yourself! I'm not going to talk to anyone who's hiding." Nothing.

I took another step forward, searching. Then the voice, again: "If you follow Me, I can help you."

This time I began to suspect. "God?" I whispered.

What should I do? "Lord?" I said, using the name Ferne sometimes used. Ferne was the one who went to church, not I. "Lord?" my voice trembled. Nothing more.

I ran back to the hotel and stumbled upstairs and opened the door, calling, "Ferne!" The light in our bedroom went on immediately. Half-packed suitcases sat on their baggage racks. "Something's happened."

I told my wife that maybe, just maybe, I had heard God speak. Actual words. About following and helping. Ferne was nodding her head up and down, saying yes, yes, even when I went on to put it more strongly: "I've met the Lord, my dear!"

The light of morning didn't quell our excitement even in the face of the same empty breakfast tables. That noon we unpacked our bags.

Over the next few days I occasionally wandered to the back of the property, where I'd met Him. What did God mean when He said He'd help? And what was the right and honorable thing to do about our debts when we had no money? These weren't exactly musings—it was more like I was talking to God, asking questions. And amazingly, it also seemed I was getting answers.

The first thing I thought the Lord told me to do was to call each of the purveyors who had been sitting in our lobby. I was to tell them I still had no money but appreciated their patience and that if I prospered they would be our suppliers for as long as I owned the hotel. Sounded like still talk to me, but I followed Him.

Next morning there was not one bill collector waiting in the lobby.

On the third day a gentleman came to the front desk. He was not one of the purveyors, but I figured he must have been from some other creditor because he said he wanted to talk about money. I barely looked up. What more could I say to these bill collectors? "You are wasting your time, sir. I have no money."

"Banks are in the business of lending money," the man said.

"That doesn't do me any good. I have no credit."

"I think we can work something out through an insurance policy."

Slowly I began to pay attention. This man was selling life insurance. He told me he had convinced the local bank that under special circumstances the Alta Mira deserved a loan, even now. All the ingredients for success were there except capital and time. Capital, for improvement. And time, for my top experience to pay off. That's where insurance came in. The bank would lend me money for improvements; the hotel would take out a policy on my life, with the bank as beneficiary; if I died early, before the bank could be repaid from profits at the hotel, the loan would be repaid from death benefits.

One week later the bank president called me and said, "Mr. Wachter, we have the privilege of offering you a loan for one hundred thousand dollars."

Ferne and I were singing with joy. We began putting our new capital to work, asking for God's guidance at each step. First we were to pay off the baker and fishmonger and butcher and greengrocer. Then bit by bit we were to landscape, and get rid of those thumping pipes.

Most exciting of all was the day we hired the contractor to start work on the terrace. I'd been right. That terrace wasn't even finished before people started flocking in. News passed by word of mouth that the Alta Mira had a wonderful outdoor area with umbrellas and flowers and a terrific view. Before we knew it we were swamped. We had to call the contractor again with plans for expanding the terrace. With the money that now started to flow through our books we refurbished the hotel itself, three rooms at a time, each with its own bath. All of the suppliers who had kept faith with us flourished too.

Nearly thirty-four years have passed since I heard the voice on our hotel grounds. Our hotel is so successful that we get dozens of offers every year to buy us out.

But at 93, where would I go and what would I do? Our church and our staff and customers are our very lives. Ferne and I thank God for this by making every effort to follow Him. Every morning over coffee we read the Bible and pray for individuals among the 50-member hotel staff. And we pray for our guests, those who come back every year and those who are about to become our friends. Above all we thank God for the privilege of following Him in these times when every day brings some new risk.

It's interesting how, when I was 20, my father became upset when I did not follow him down the safe and known way. Years later my heavenly Father also told me to follow Him. But He added the words which have let me see risk as adventure: "Follow Me," He said, "and I will help you."   *March 1992*